Against All Odds

Famous and Infamous Women of China & Some Contemporary Achievers 220 BC - 1995 AD

by
Molly Phillips

I hope you enjoy these life stories

Molly Phillips

Printed in British Columbia, Canada

Cover painting: Li Xing Bai
Book design, typesetting, graphics: Roy Diment (Vivencia Resources Group), Victoria, B.C., Canada

Canadian Cataloguing in Publication Data

Phillips, Molly, 1909-
  Against all odds

  Includes bibliographical references.
  ISBN 1-55212-381-2

  1. Women--China--Biography. I. Title.
DS734.P54 2000   920.72'0951   C00-910563-8

TRAFFORD

This book was published *on-demand* in cooperation with Trafford Publishing.
On-demand publishing is a unique process and service of making a book available for retail sale to the public taking advantage of on-demand manufacturing and Internet marketing. **On-demand publishing** includes promotions, retail sales, manufacturing, order fulfilment, accounting and collecting royalties on behalf of the author.

Suite 6E, 2333 Government St., Victoria, B.C. V8T 4P4, CANADA

Phone	250-383-6864	Toll-free	1-888-232-4444 (Canada & US)
Fax	250-383-6804	E-mail	sales@trafford.com
Web site	www.trafford.com	TRAFFORD PUBLISHING IS A DIVISION OF TRAFFORD HOLDINGS LTD.	
Trafford Catalogue #00-0045		www.trafford.com/robots/00-0045.html	

10   9   8   7   6   5   4   3

Contents

Foreword

The author of this book, Molly Phillips, was born in Hong Kong in 1909. Her father, Sidney Frank Ricketts, an electrical engineer, was sent out by his firm in Britain in 1903 to build the first electric powerhouse in Canton. Her mother, Ruth Lavinia Briscombe a teacher, was appointed by the British Wesleyan Methodist Church to serve in Canton as a teacher. The couple met in Canton and were married there in 1908. When the powerhouse was completed, Sidney's firm moved him to Hong Kong and in October 1909, Molly was born. She was named Mary but as the Cantonese have no R sound in their language, the Chinese name for Mary was pronounced Mahlay, which very soon became Molly and by that name she is best known. When the Revolution of 1911 occurred, life in China was so chaotic that it was impossible to do business with Chinese firms. Consequently the Ricketts family emigrated to Canada where Molly was brought up and educated. After completing her university degree in 1929 she continued her studies in teacher training at which time she met her future husband, Richard Gaundry Phillips. But the great depression made it impossible to find a job. Molly was offered a three year teaching position in Canton and she and her fiancé agreed that she should accept and when she returned surely Richard (Dick) would have work. But five months after Molly arrived in Canton a teaching position opened for Dick also in Canton and he immediately accepted. When Molly completed her contract, they were married in Canton and later moved to Hong Kong when Dick's teaching position was transferred to that city. Two boys were born to them in Hong Kong and in January 1939 they returned to Vancouver on leave, but with the outbreak of World War II in August of 1939 they were unable to return to the Orient.

It was not until 1974 that the way opened up for Molly to take a group of friends to China and from that time until the mid 1990's Molly managed 26 trips to China, 22 as leader of tour groups, one to the International

Tourist Convention in Beijing, one to teach at Yantai University summer school, one as a guest of the province of Shandong, and one to explore possible inter-university relations for the Federation of Canada-China Friendship Associations which had been formed in 1980 to unite the fifteen associations that had organized across Canada.

Her life in China and her many tours to nearly every province gave Molly a wealth of information. Her first book, *I Saw Three Chinas*, is an historical autobiography of the family from the early 1900's to 1990 when the book was published and is now sold out. The three China's were the imperial era of the Ching dynasty when the author was born, the republican era in the 1930's when military leaders such as Cheung Kai-shek headed the government, and finally the modern era after the revolution of 1949. Lately her interest particularly in the women of China, has led her to make a study of outstanding women who have played important roles in the political and cultural life of their country. This book Against All Odds is the outcome of her study.

Acknowledgments

My very grateful thanks to artist Li Xing Bai for the portrait on the front cover of the book, and for three paintings that have been reduced to black and white figures to illustrate women featured in the book. Thanks also to the Chinese Women's Federation who arranged for me to interview the "contemporary achievers" in Beijing, and the minority women at the Institute of Managerial Cadres of Women. Thanks too to the women themselves who gave of their time to tell me of their lives and work. I would also like to acknowledge the care and cooperation of Roy Diment in designing the book and preparing it for publication. Thanks also to my sons for their support and suggestions, and friends who photographed or found pictures for illustrations.

Chapter 1

Sacrificial Love
Meng Jiangnu

Figurine of Meng Jiangnu

At Shawniguan at the extreme eastern end of the Great Wall is a temple dedicated to the memory of Meng Jiangnu. Her statue presides over a small hall where pilgrims, mostly women, come bearing flowers and fruit to honour her memory. Her story is a strange and tragic one.

When Qin Shi Huang, the first Emperor of China, completed his conquest of the six surrounding states in 221 BC and set up the united kingdom, he began fortifying his boundaries against the marauding nomadic people of the north. Joining together the many sections of walls that each state had built, he began the stupendous task of building what has become known as the Great Wall.

Half a million conscripts were seized and sent to labour on the prodigious task. Among them was Meng Jiangnu's husband, Wan Xiliang. How they met and married has been the subject of poetry, folklore and opera. The most romantic scene is that as she walked in the garden of her home one day she was startled by a man jumping over the wall.

"Refuge," he implored. "I have escaped from the press gang."

Jiangnu led him into the house and her family agreed to harbour him. In true romantic style they fell in love and were married. But happiness was not to be theirs. On the night of their wedding the imperial officials discovered Wan's whereabouts, entered the home, and seized him.

Legend has it that as they parted Jiangnu hastily pulled a white jade pin from her upswept hair and broke it in two. Giving half to Wan she cried:

"My heart is as pure and white as this jade. If you keep this half you will know that I am always beside you." Then with tears of anguish she bade farewell to her husband as he was wrenched from her.

As time passed, the horror stories surrounding the building of the wall reached the people. The ruthless overseers exacted a heavy toll. Thousands died from brutal treatment and inhuman conditions. Ancient records bear witness to piles of corpses left to rot, and skeletons buried within the Great Wall itself.

No news of her husband reached Jaingnu. As spring approached she longed for him. Walking in the garden she saw the peach trees blossom and the birds mating and building their nests. She was conscious of her own solitariness and sang her sad songs, overwhelmed with grieving and desolation.

Summer passed and as winter approached she was deeply concerned. Did he have warm clothing or a suitable place to live? Was the work too strenuous for him? Was he being mistreated? Her distress became so great that she decided to go in search of him and find out for herself how he was faring. She quickly sewed some padded clothes and shoes and set out on her long and arduous journey.

She trudged along the roads, climbed mountains, threaded her way through valleys and crossed rivers, stopping to rest wherever kind villagers offered her hospitality.

One night, far from any habitation, she slept out-of-doors, only to find herself next morning covered with a blanket of snow. On another occasion, sleeping in a grove of trees, she dreamed that her husband was coming to meet her. But her happiness was short lived for he told her that he was no longer alive. Undaunted she continued her journey, not knowing which way to go. According to legend a crow flew down and cawed, then rose and alighted further along the way, cawing as if to lead her on. She took this as an omen and followed the bird, and as she walked she sang of the thick snow, of her burden of winter clothes for her husband, and of only a crow to guide her to the far distant Great Wall where she hoped to find her husband.

Finally, after months of travel, she glimpsed the outlines of the Wall, snaking its way over mountains and through valleys as far as the eye could see. Shivering in the bitter cold were the men, digging foundations, laying rock upon rock. Overseers drove the slave labourers, lashing with whips the pitiful men who had been impressed by the Emperor for his mighty construction.

Meng Jiangnu followed the Wall, viewing with horror the dead unburied bodies lying where they had fallen. The emaciated workers could give her no information about her husband until one day she learned that Wan Xiliang had died many months ago and his bones lay under the Wall where he had collapsed.

Hearing the tragic story, Meng Jaingnu fainted and lay unconscious for some time. When she finally revived, she wept in grief for days, moving those around her to join with her in her lamentations.

At this point of time a large section of the Wall collapsed, revealing the bones of Wan Xiliang and the half jade hairpin that she had given him.

"It is Meng Jiangnu's tears that have brought down the Wall," cried the people, and their hatred of the cruel Emperor exploded.

It is said that when the Emperor heard this story he journeyed to the site to see this woman who had such a powerful influence that the Wall collapsed in response to her mournful laments. According to legend, the Emperor found her to be a beautiful woman and wished to take her as a concubine. Loathing the Emperor as she did, she nevertheless consented on condition that her husband should be buried in a golden coffin, that the royal court should attend the funeral, and that the Emperor himself should attend, wearing mourning clothes. So impressed was the Emperor by her beauty and spirit that he agreed to her demands.

But no sooner was the funeral procession over than Meng Jiangnu threw herself into the ocean from the rock point where the Great Wall began. Impressed by her fidelity the local people venerated her and raised a shrine in her honour. Today a small temple with her statue stands at Shawniguan, in memory of a woman whose love was immortal, and who represented to her people the embodiment of hatred of cruelty and oppression.

Statue of Meng Jiangnu and attendants in Shanhaiguan Temple

Temple honouring Meng Jiangnu at Shanhaiguan at the east end of the Great Wall

Chapter 2

Dream Maiden (Part 1)
Wang Chao Chun

Figurine of Wang Chao Chun

Wang Ch'iang peeped through the circular archway that led into the courtyard. The bright sun made more enticing the red persimmons that hung in abundance on the potted trees. She ventured out and made her way along the smooth stone walk between the fruit trees.

Not far behind her appeared Ching, her waiting maid, adoring as always her young mistress. Ching was convinced that Ch'iang was the most beautiful girl in Hubei province.

Ch'iang saw her maid and called her to pick a persimmon. Then nibbling the sweet fruit she sat on the bench and drew from the folds of her flowing dress a book of poetry. For Ch'iang was not only beautiful but intelligent and well educated. Her father, a scholar who had been appointed around 50 BC to an official position in the Zigui county government, loved his beautiful daughter and saw to it that her inquiring mind was given the opportunity to study the arts and read the history and literature of her people.

A rustle in the flowerbed attracted Ch'iang's attention. She reached down to her side and lifted out her white kitten who had been dozing in the sun-drench garden. Ch'iang rose and, carrying her kitten, sauntered through the garden, circling the small pool in the centre. She watched the miniature orange carp that darted through the water and wondered if the little fish in their small pond felt as restricted as she sometimes did.

As she strolled she recalled that her mother had intimated to her that as she was approaching her sixteenth birthday they would have to call in the matchmaker to arrange for her betrothal. Ch'iang hoped that it would not fall to her lot to be engaged to a rich old man looking for a young wife. She wondered if there was an eligible young man in the district who might be willing to give her some freedom to enjoy life.

After the evening meal Ch'iang was called by her father to talk with him. She wondered if this was to be the beginning of betrothal arrangements, but she was hardly prepared for her father's disclosure. Sorrowfully he told her,

"The Emperor has sent an emissary to discover and bring to the royal court the most beautiful girls in Hubei province, and you have been summoned to attend."

'Why have I been chosen?" she asked in surprise.

Her father looked at his beautiful daughter. "Your beauty is known in these parts," he explained, "and word has reached the royal emissary."

Although Ch'iang held in great respect the Son of Heaven, the Emperor Yuan Ti, she recoiled at the idea of becoming one of the hundreds of concubines that made up the Emperor's seraglio.

"Please, father, I do not want to go," she pleaded.

Her father looked at her thoughtfully and wondered what would be the emissary's reaction to a refusal. He soon discovered. He was summoned to the Governor's house.

"I have been told that your work has not been very satisfactory of late," he was told. "When you passed the examinations so successfully we expected better results."

Wang was dumbfounded. His work had never before been questioned.

"What is the nature of the complaints?" he asked.

"I do not know," said the Governor. "but I was asked to warn you that you must improve your attitude if you wish to retain your position."

Wang returned to his home to consider the rebuke "Improve your attitude." Could this have something to do with his refusal to allow his daughter to be taken off to Chang'an to the royal court?

He returned to his office to complete the documents he was preparing and was met with a cold reception. The head of the department was abrupt and uncommunicative. The other scholars with whom he worked were aloof.

When Wang arrived home he found his servants disgruntled. They had had difficulty in procuring daily supplies and had received surly answers to their inquiries. Ching had been accosted on the street and suggestions made that her master was working against the Emperor and might be tried for anti-imperial activities.

It became obvious that the royal emissary had set in motion the wheels of persecution.

Wang was filled with grief. How could be tell his daughter? If he was dismissed in disgrace from office on false charges, how could he support his family?

Ch'iang saw that her father was troubled and finally elicited from the servants the source of his grief. She went to her father immediately.

"I wish to beg forgiveness for being such a wilful daughter," she said. "I have reconsidered my answer to the royal emissary. I will go with him to the royal court."

Wang was stricken. The loss of his beautiful daughter was the price he must pay for his position and his family's security.

"In losing our daughter," he lamented, "We have no one to cheer us in our old age."

"Do not be sorrowful, father," said Ch'iang. "Perhaps I shall be able to make a place for myself in the Emperor's court and bring glory to my ancestors. If I win imperial favour I will beg the Emperor to bring my parents to live in the capital to share my honour."

When the emissary was informed of the girl's decision, hasty preparations were made for her journey. There was little time as the royal envoy was eager to be on his way with the nearly five hundred girls he had gathered from the district, with Ch'iang whom he considered as his prize. Although he had been warned by the Emperor not to accept tributes or bribes, the wily emissary had extracted handsome presents of silver and gold from the families as expressions of appreciation for his presenting their daughters to the Emperor. With the fortune he had amassed he looked forward to a future life of ease.

On the day of her departure Ch'iang burned incense, kneeling at the family shrine and offering prayers before the tablets of her ancestors. Then the servants gathered to pay their respects to the young mistress they loved, while her parents stood stolidly by the gateway. Wrapped in her light cloak to protect her from the wind and dust of the journey, Ch'iang emerged into the courtyard, her kitten in her arms. Turning to Ching she placed her pet in the girl's arms.

"Take care of her for me," was all Ch'iang said, but Ching saw her mistress's lip quiver as she handed over the kitten. Then Ch'iang turned and walked to her waiting parents. With downcast eyes she bowed low, murmuring her respectful farewell, then walked resolutely through the archway to the waiting carriage.

Ch'iang climbed into the conveyance and the carriage assistant pulled the curtains around her. She was beginning her journey into a strange new world.

The long procession wound its way over land and river, skirting the distant mountains, passing lakes and rivers that swarmed with wild ducks, glimpsing the farmers in their green rice fields or the herdsmen as they shepherded their flocks of sheep and goats. Ch'iang was conceded by all the company to be the most beautiful of all the girls but her gentleness and kindness overcame any feelings of jealousy that might have arisen.

After a month of travel the weary travellers arrived about 40 BC at the royal capital of Chang'an. As the entourage passed through the gates of the city wall, the palaces and magnificent gardens, the towers and pavilions, lakes and parks of the imperial city came into view. Officials came to greet the party and the envoy presented himself to the Emperor in the Purple Palace.

The envoy, Mao Yen-shou, the court painter and a powerful figure, had slyly insinuated himself into the good graces of Emperor Yuan Ti. When the Emperor had had a dream of a very beautiful maiden, he had sent Mao to bring the most beautiful girls he could find in the hope that his dream maiden would be among them. When the large retinue of girls arrived at the palace they were housed in the various chambers in the Inner Court, and Mao was ordered to paint two portraits of each girl so that the Emperor could choose his favourite.

Mao realized that Ch'iang surpassed all the other beauties he had gathered, and he felt assured that she would rank first in the Emperor's eyes. Her name at court had been changed to Chao Chan, meaning Brilliant Lady. After the first portrait was painted Mao sent one of his henchmen to suggest to Chao Chun that she should present four hundred ounces of gold as an expression of appreciation to the artist. But Chao Chun did not respond. When Mao came to make the second painting Chao Chan was arrayed in an exquisite "rose brocade dress, with phoenix shaped hairpins set with pearls, jade and coral earrings and golden bracelets." When after five days the painting was finished, Mao praised her beauty but Chao Chun made no offer of a bribe. She considered that Mao was paid by the Emperor for his work, and with her own concept of honesty and virtue she would not stoop to bribery.

Once again Mao sent one of his hirelings to urge her to present a gift to the painter, but she disregarded his suggestion. Again she was approached with the suggestion that her future depended on the artist's portrayal, but Chao Chun indicated that her father had already given the painter a handsome gift and she had nothing to offer. Her Confucian beliefs would not permit her to encourage the artist to paint too flattering a portrait, which would be a dishonourable deception. The messenger returned empty handed and Mao was furious. His dignity was affronted and he decided that she would pay the penalty. Beneath her right eye in both portraits he painted a black mole.

When Mao had finished all the portraits he presented them to Yuan Ti. The Emperor was not attracted to any until he saw Chao Chun. He recognized in her the embodiment of his dream maiden and asked to see her. Mao was distraught. Prostrating himself before the Emperor he pointed out that the black mole was a sign of ill-omen and foretold danger to the safety of the Emperor's sacred person and the safety of the state. He begged the Emperor to put the woman away for the sake of the peace and security of the nation. The Emperor, never doubting the loyalty of the painter, admitted that the black mole was a danger sign but saw no harm in just having a look at the girl. Mao was terrified. Knocking his head on the floor, he begged his sovereign not to run the risk of even bringing this woman into his presence. Moved by Mao's supposed concern for the safety of his person and of the nation, Yuan Ti finally ordered that Chao Chun be transferred to the Cold Palace. Mao's staff was sworn to secrecy, and the Emperor's superstitious fears denied him the joy of receiving the enchanting dream maiden for whom he had long yearned.

Chao Chun was mystified at her incarceration in the Cold Palace. When the servants began to hint that other less beautiful girls were being received by the Emperor while she passed her days in cold seclusion, she still kept her hopes high that one day she would be summoned into the sacred presence of the Emperor whom she greatly revered. But the summons never came. Eventually the old gatekeeper, moved by her unhappiness, gave Chao Chun a pipa, and she was able to play the instrument and sing her plaintive songs of love and loneliness.

Meanwhile, the Emperor, while enjoying the ladies of the Court, still longed for his dream maiden. One evening while strolling in the garden he heard Chao Chun singing. Moved by the beautiful sound he asked an attendant where this lovely melody came from. The attendant, one of Mao's henchmen, warned the Emperor that its melancholy nature portended evil and was distasteful to those who heard it. The Emperor's belief in omens was such that he did not pursue his interest further. Many of the girls, the palace guards, and even some of the princes knew the truth about Chao Chun but Mao's power had so corrupted the court that none dared to tell the truth.

Fortunately for Chao Chun another girl called Li Wan-hua, because of her strict principles had also refused to bribe the painter, and she too was passing her days in cold seclusion. Knowing that her charm was in no way equal to some of the other beauties, Wan-hua spent her days reading, painting, embroidering and practising the art of calligraphy. She loved Chao Chun and there blossomed a warm and lasting friendship. Wan-hua, overhearing some of the eunuchs discussing the reasons for Chao Chun's plight, reported their conversation to Chao Chun who was stricken with anguish at the news. That Mao should have deceived the Emperor and ruined her life was almost unbearable, but she was strengthened in the knowledge that her own name remained pure and her life chaste.

But Chao Chun could not refrain from grief. "Why was I born with the gift of beauty?" she cried. "Why must the Son of Heaven be deceived by this disloyal official?" Why have I no hope or right to seek justice and restitution? At home I was loved and cherished and now I am cut off from my loving parents." Her tears and anguish perturbed Wan-hua.

"Do not let your beauty be destroyed by grief and despair," she begged. "Heaven may yet smile on you if you face life with courage."

"Your words comfort me," said Chao Chun. "I thank you for your wise counsel. Heaven has sent you to me."

The girls swore eternal friendship and together passed three years in companionship. Chao Chun at times pined in her solitude and felt humiliated by the neglect and lack of gaiety in her life. Sometimes her loneliness and sense of having been forsaken resulted in illness. Her heart cried out for love and recognition, but Wan-hua's constant care helped her to retain her natural beauty and to believe that some day greatness would come to her. Little did she anticipate the form in which this greatness would come.

Wang Chao Chun by Li Xing Bai

*Statue of Wang Chao Chun and the Khan in the
park dedicated to her in the capital of Mongolia*

Chapter 3

Dream Maiden (Part 2)
Wang Chao Chun

*Scroll of Wang Chao Chun & The Khan
(Mongolian ruler)*

While Chao Chun languished in seclusion important developments were unfolding within the empire. For several hundred years barbarian tribes, particularly those known as the Hsiung-nu, had been terrorizing the northern provinces of China. They were a nomadic people who shifted from place to place with their flocks and herds in search of fresh pastures. An illiterate people, they had no written language, communicating entirely by word of mouth. They did not engage in agricultural pursuits, nor did they have any permanent settlements.

The Hsiung-nu were renowned for their excellent horsemanship and were honoured by their leaders for bravery, but despised and punished for any sign of cowardice or weakness. Their skill with weapons, the speed of their horses, and their merciless attacks gained them a reputation as ruthless conquerors. War was for them a profession and plundering their means of support, apart from the animal flesh of their flocks and the milk of the mares and goats. China's wealth incited them to make incursions into the empire which led to the building of the Great Wall in 214 BC.

But in spite of the wall, in 202 BC the barbarians ravaged one of the northern provinces, China was defeated, and the Emperor was forced to sue for peace. An alliance was arranged whereby China would make an annual grant to the tribe of silk, wine and food and a lady of royal blood would be given in marriage to the Khan, the tribal leader. When the Empress objected to her daughter being given in marriage in this fashion, it was agreed that an attractive maiden from the Emperor's seraglio would be substituted and given the status of princess.

As time passed the Hsiung-nu became less successful in their attacks and by 68 BC the Khan, weakened by defeats, decided to co-operate with the Emperor, and one of his sons was sent as a hostage-page to the Chinese Court. The Khan volunteered his warriors as frontier guards and eventually offered to pay homage to the Emperor. Spectacular visits and state ceremonies cemented the entente and in BC 48, when Yuan Ti ascended the throne of China, the Khan himself visited the royal court in Ch'ang-an. He was much impressed with the singing and dancing girls, the musicians, and the beautiful women. As an honoured guest he revelled in the luxury of the sumptuous surroundings, the entertainment, the choice food, and the splendour of court life.

As the years passed the Khan decided that the time had come to establish a blood relationship with the Chinese imperial line. Early in the year 33 BC ministers of the Khan, bearing gold, valuable fur skins, and a hundred horses, arrived in Ch'ang-an with the Khan's request that a lady of the imperial court be sent as a bride to strengthen the bonds of peace.

Yuan Ti let it be known that such an alliance was contemplated and the women of his seraglio were terrified at the idea of being exiled to the unknown grasslands of the north and the unsophisticated life of the barbarian nomads.

Chao Chun, however, bored with the empty life she was leading saw an opportunity to serve her Emperor and perhaps contribute to the peace and security of her country. To the amazement and horror of her court friends she volunteered to go. The Emperor, although impressed by her courageous attitude on behalf of her country and her sovereign, nevertheless welcomed the opportunity to be rid of the girl with the inauspicious mole and the sad songs.

A month of planning was necessary for festivities befitting a woman who was to become a queen. Chao Chun was raised to imperial rank with the title Yung-an Kung-chu Princess of Eternal Peace, an unanticipated foreshadowing of her future role.

Elaborate preparations were made for a feast. The palace was decorated, the Empress and Princesses, other members of the royal family and the highest ranking nobles were ordered to appear in their finest robes to attend the festivities. During all the time when preparations were being made, Mao, the court painter, was ill and being absent from the court was unaware of events.

On the day of the feast the whole assembly waited with intense expectation for the approach of the bride-to-be. Arrayed in a spectacular gown of crimson, embroidered with dragons and trimmed with scintillating jewels, she was led into the glittering hall by ladies-in-waiting carrying lanterns. The breathless assembly marvelled that the Emperor would allow such a radiant beauty to be given in marriage to a barbarian Khan. The Khan's envoy was so delighted that he assumed the Emperor must fear the Khan's power if he was willing to part with such a divine creature. Courtiers who were not familiar with Chao Chun's story were amazed that the Son of Heaven would send away so precious a jewel.

Ensconced on his Dragon Throne, Yuan Ti sat stunned. Here was the Dream Maiden, the flawless beauty, for whom he had waited over the years, and she was pledged to a barbarian ruler. No mole or scar disfigured her face. How could he redress the wrong and claim her for himself? Ardently he expressed his intention to redress the cruel wrong that had been done, and to find another maiden to replace her.

But Chao Chun begged him not to jeopardize the friendship that had been built up between the two nations. She assured her Royal Sovereign that she could not enjoy happiness when it would undoubtedly bring invasion and disaster to her country. Yuan Ti could not but admire the girl who was willing to sacrifice herself for the safety of himself and the nation. But his anger was unbridled as he thought of the perfidy of the artist Mao. Troops were sent immediately to arrest the artist who was summarily executed. The populace, while mourning the fate of Chao Chun, rejoiced at the justice of Mao's fate.

Yuan Ti's deliberation with his ministers confirmed the decision that Chao Chun must go to the Khan. All feared the vengeance and hostilities that would ensue if the pledge of the princess was revoked.

Chao Chun begged his sacred Majesty to allow her to depart, thanking him for his gracious concern for her and entreating him to devote his life to the future welfare of her dearly beloved fatherland. Her only request was that Li Wan-hua be allowed to accompany her, and this modest petition was readily granted.

Elaborate preparations were made for the journey to the northern realm. Early in the spring Chao Chun left with a spectacular procession. The royal chariot inlaid with lacquer and decorated with elegant hangings, was escorted by mounted Mongolian warriors and special Chinese envoys. Costly gifts of rare gems, carved ivory and musical instruments inlaid with precious stones made up some of the baggage that was loaded on to horses and mules and would later be transferred to Mongolian camels.

On the day of the departure a bitter wind blew and a storm lashed the entourage as if Heaven itself was outraged. But Chao Chun, wrapped in her rich cape lined with white fox fur, and her satin headpiece trimmed with sable, bravely bade farewell to her homeland and set out on the wearying journey to her northern home. Uncertain as to the life and customs of the people over whom she would reign as queen, Chao Chun could only surmise what life among her nomadic subjects would be like

After a month and a half the cavalcade reached the Jade Pass through the snow-capped mountains. The nights were cold, but the elegant bronze brazier and sacks of coal that the Emperor had sent for the well-being of his Dream Maiden, and the soft skins and warm rugs provided by the Khan's company, kept Chao Chun and her companion, Li Wan-hua, warm and comfortable.

Chao Chun had long since given up the lurching chariot for the stately black and white steed sent by the Khan for his bride. After three months of trekking, the party reached the Gobi desert with its endless expanse of sand and barren landscapes. At this point the Chinese guards returned to Ch'ang-an and the cavalcade continued for many hundreds of miles. A dispatch rider was sent to inform the Khan that the party would soon be arriving and Chao Chun and Wan-hua looked forward to the end of the long and very arduous journey.

The Khan was exultant when he heard the news of the successful expedition to the Han royal court. The envoy that had negotiated the compact was generously rewarded with gold, cattle and promotion to a high rank, and was enjoined to make preparations for a brilliant wedding ceremony.

When the people heard that a royal bride from the Imperial Court was soon to arrive, feasting and merrymaking were the order of the day.

The Khan waited impatiently for the caravan's arrival and prepared a magnificent escort to greet Chao Chun and her attendants. As she stepped from the special chariot sent to carry her the last short distance, the Khan was overwhelmed by her charm and delicate beauty. He could hardly believe that he, a fierce nomadic warrior, had been so favoured by the Han Emperor. His heart went out to the beautiful Chinese princess who was to be his bride.

Chao Chun and her waiting maids were ushered into a luxurious yurt (tent) that was to be her home. It was circular with a light wooden frame covered with camels' hair felt, approximately thirty feet in diameter. A carved altar with golden candlesticks, incense burners and wine cups stood at one end, and a large couch covered with quilts and cushions doubled as seating during the day and a bed at night. Rugs and fur skins covered the floor and beautifully designed chests and cupboards brought from Ch'ang-an were arranged around the room.

The strain of the journey and the strange new land and customs left Chao Chun exhausted, but her Chinese maids and her friend Wan-hua poured out their love for her in tender ministrations and saw that her spirits were revived. Chao Chun's interest in her surroundings soon sparked a desire to understand the customs and habits of those who were to be her subjects, and she made every attempt to satisfy the unending inquisitiveness of the women and children who were always eager to see and watch her. Her gentleness and kindness won their hearts, and her tact and discretion in dealing with the ladies of the Court created an atmosphere of friendliness that boded well for the future.

As the wedding day approached there were feverish preparations for a celebration unparalleled in this northern land. The grand yurt that was the royal residence was impressive as colourful banners, carvings, furs and embroidered hangings decorated the hall that served as the Khan's throne room. Thousands of cattle and sheep arrived as gifts, and musicians performed the haunting music of Mongolia.

Finally the propitious day arrived and Chao Chun, arrayed in a dazzling bridal dress and escorted by a dozen bridesmaids, entered the Grand Yurt where the Khan stood waiting. Military and civil officials were arraigned at the altar to assist in the rituals, and as the Master of Ceremonies escorted the royal couple to worship Heaven and Earth, the strange wedding music burst forth. At the conclusion of the observances the bride was escorted to the bridal chamber attended by Wan-hua who was now her senior lady-in-waiting. Meanwhile festivities in the banquet tent were unrestrained and the Khan in an unusual gesture mixed and rejoiced with his courtiers. But his desire to see his divine bride led him to withdraw quietly from the celebrations and make his way to the bridal chamber. He was overcome by Chao Chun's undreamed of loveliness, and the imperious ruler of the Hsiung-nu nomads felt moved to adoration and desire to offer himself and his kingdom to her.

Chao Chun, unnerved by her husband's passion and the strangeness of the primitive setting, was visibly distraught. Realizing her anxiety the Khan assured her that in spite of the differences in customs and manners, he wished only to serve her and he begged her not to be unhappy.

Chao Chun, moved by his expression of concern, promised that if the Khan would pledge his undying loyalty to her homeland, she would be a dutiful wife. Succumbing to her nearness, the Khan drew her to him with tender caresses and whispers of love.

So great was the Khan's love for Chao Chun that he did everything in his power to dispel her feelings of homesickness and to surround her with furnishings and attendants from her homeland. Chao Chun, for her part, was determined to accept the Khan and his people and to exhibit a keen interest in their welfare. The common people came to love their kind-hearted queen, and the manners of the Court were vastly improved by Chao Chun's presence and her willingness to instruct the ladies in the arts.

Athletic meets were always a source of delight to the people and Chao Chun accompanied her husband on these occasions, which pleased the populace and won their hearts. The Khan arranged for women who were expert riders to instruct her in horsemanship, archery, hunting and other forms of martial arts.

On occasions when court cases were held and the Khan's word was law, Chao Chun was able to temper the decisions and win freedom or lesser punishments for those under arrest. Subtly she influenced the proud warrior to govern in a kindlier and less extravagant way, which resulted in a more peaceful and contented land. Good relations existed between the Imperial Court and their nomadic neighbours so that the northern borders remained free of conflict.

After a year had passed there was great rejoicing when a son was born to the royal couple. Congratulations, presents and festivities celebrated the coming of an heir to the throne, and Chao Chun, fascinated by the baby, set her mind to mould a worthy successor to the Khan. The child was active and healthy and two years went by in peace and prosperity.

But the Khan was not a young man and one day when he was hunting he was overcome with dizziness. The best medical advisers were summoned but by the following morning it was evident that his illness was fatal. His state councillors were summoned and it was announced that the oldest son of one of his previous wives would succeed to the throne. After this pronouncement his last words were for the safety and care of his beloved Chinese queen. In 31 BC after reigning for twenty-eight years, the valiant old warrior died and Chao Chun at twenty-two years of age was left a widow.

Bereft of the devotion of her husband and longing to return to her homeland and her parents, Chao Chun pondered her future. After the royal funeral rites were concluded she was shocked to learn that according to tribal custom the new Khan wished to take over his father's seraglio and to make the beautiful Chinese widow his chief queen. Chao Chun insisted that the Khan wait until she received instructions from the Han Emperor and immediately a messenger was dispatched to Ch'ang-an. The Emperor Yuan Ti had died and his son simply replied that she should conform to the customs of the Hsiung-mu.

"How can I do this?" wept Chao Chun as she conferred with her dear friend and confidant Wan-hua. "The teachings of Confucius would abhor such a relationship."

"If you refuse," counselled Wan-hua, "your son's life may be at stake."

"Not only my son's life but the peace between our two countries is at stake," admitted Chao Chun. "I must accept for the sake of my homeland and my child."

The new Khan was delighted with Chao Chun's decision and she was immediately declared his lawful wife and Queen. He had long admired and secretly loved the beautiful young woman and he proclaimed weeks of feasting and celebrations to honour their marriage. So ardent was his love and concern that Chao Chun was gradually able to respond with affection, and her kindness and generosity maintained a harmonious spirit among the other women of the court. At her marriage she had secured the promise of the Khan's continued allegiance to China and the maintenance of peace along the borders.

Within a year Chao Chun gave birth to a daughter and the Khan was so overjoyed that he decided to choose a new site with a magnificent view to build a comfortable home for his family. Another daughter was born a year later and Chao Chun was intent on bringing up her children with the same sense of loyalty and consideration for others that had characterized her own life. Her influence on her husband also led to more merciful dealings with enemies and the inculcation of a sense of justice in the affairs of state.

As the years passed, Chao Chun's three children grew to adulthood and the elder daughter was sent as a lady-in-waiting to the Empress Dowager in Ch'ang-an and the second girl married a Tartar Minister of State. Meanwhile the son, an ardent hunter and skilled in horsemanship, trained in Chinese classics by his mother, and imbued with Chao Chun's respect for justice and devotion to his people, looked forward to the day when he might rightfully succeed to the throne.

The death of the Khan was followed by a succesion of rulers until in AD 18 the sixth Khan decided to rid himself of all possible rivals. Chao Chun's son was murdered, and when the news was brought to his mother, she collapsed. Life lost its meaning, her spirit was broken, and she died shortly afterwards.

The whole realm mourned the death of this woman they had come to love and respect. For nearly two thousand years poems and songs, stories and plays about this beloved queen have been part of the legendary history of both China and Mongolia. Her actual resting place is not known but in Hohhot, the capital of Inner Mongolia, is the best known memorial mound where statues of her and her first Khan overlook a park dedicated to her honour. Part of the park is a man-made hill topped by a pagoda consecrated to the woman whose unselfish love cemented the bonds of peace between the northern tribes and the Han empire, and whose gracious life made her revered for her justice and kindness.

Mongolian people have a saying that on her memorial hill the grass is always green. Perhaps this is the origin of the Chinese proverb "the tree of friendship is always green."

Chapter 4

Ruthless Usurper Empress Wu

Empress Wu
portrait courtesy of Li Xing Bai
leading contemporary painter

Wu Tse T'ien is unique in Chinese history. She was the only woman ever to reign as head of state. Other women before and since held power as empress dowagers or ruled through child emperors, but none have ever usurped the throne, changed the name of the dynasty and assumed the imperial powers.

In the year 638 AD the emperor T'ai Tsung heard of Wu Tse Tien's beauty and at 13 years of age she was summoned to the imperial court. Her mother was deeply distressed. Although the Emperor had just lost his Empress, he had a large harem and fourteen sons by his wife and concubines. There seemed little hope that Tse T'ien would ever hold any important place in the royal household. But the girl was not distraught.

"I may be invited into the presence of the Son of Heaven," she said. "What happiness that will be."

On arrival at the court she was given the rank of Concubine of the Fifth Grade with the title of "Elegant", and her name became Wu Chao. Above her ranked four ladies of the first Grade, nine each of the Second, Third, Fourth and Fifth Grades, all of whom were recognized as concubines for the satisfaction of the Emperor. Their day-to-day duties consisted of caring for the Empress's needs, preparing the elements for sacrifices, entertaining guests, improving their own accomplishments in singing, dancing and playing instruments, and becoming familiar with the literary works favoured by the court. Below these women were twenty-seven each in the Sixth, Seventh and Eighth Grades who were considered handmaidens with more humble duties, but were part of the Emperor's harem.

In 643 the Emperor decided to appoint an heir apparent and chose the youngest of his Empress's sons. Before long the Emperor's health began to deteriorate and Wu Chao ruthlessly set herself to cultivate the attention of the Crown Prince. When he was attending the Emperor on his sick bed Wu Chao made advances and the Crown Prince fell in love with her.

When the Emperor finally died in 649 Wu Chao together with all the other concubines had to leave the palace and enter a nunnery as was the custom of the day. At 24 years of age she had to look forward to a lifetime of seclusion since former concubines were forbidden to participate in public life. The Crown prince had had a harem of his own and the chief concubine, Lady Wang, was made Empress at his accession. But Lady Wang was childless and was alarmed at the increasing favours shown to her rivals. To counteract this favouritism she looked for a way out.

At this point the young Emperor, Kao-tsung, on the anniversary of his father's death, went to the convent seemingly to participate in a ceremony to pay his filial respects. There he saw Wu Chao and his love for her was renewed. Lady Wang became aware of this attraction and saw in it the answer to her dilemma. She encouraged Wu Chao to prepare herself for a return to the palace and persuaded the young Emperor to bring the girl back. Little did she suspect that her own jealousy would lead to cataclysmic events.

In 654 after the Emperor brought Wu Chao back to the palace she began a rapid rise in importance. She gave birth to a son and later to a daughter who died at birth or was surreptitiously smothered by Wu Chao. When the Emperor came to visit the mother and child, Wu Chao evinced great distress when it was discovered that the child was dead and because

Empress Wang had just visited the infant, the death was laid at her door. The Empress was thereupon deposed and Wu Chao was eventually raised to the position of Empress.

The discredited Empress and the chief concubine were imprisoned in the inner palace and eventually cruelly tortured and fearfully killed. All those who owed their positions to the former Empress or who had supported her were degraded, sent to posts in far parts of the country or were imprisoned or killed for often trumped up charges. Censors whose duty it was to report disloyal acts were torn between duty and fear of incurring danger to their families. Charges were brought against the Supreme Commander of the Army and other elder statesmen, resulting in exile, suicide or execution.

In 656 Wu Chao's position was further strengthened by the birth of her second son and shortly afterwards the former Crown Prince was denounced. Fearing for his life, he became deranged. His strange behaviour was used as a pretext to remove him from the Court and he was exiled with the status of a commoner.

Emperor Kao-tsung suffered from apoplexy and Wu Chao became his able assistant, reading documents and issuing decisions in his name. Although history largely records the calamities and terrors of the period, there is little doubt that the Empress was a successful director of many important enterprises. A long war with Korea ended in complete victory for China which added further to the prestige of the Emperor and the Empress who assumed credit for the outcome.

Wu Chao undoubtedly had the capability for administration and it was she who conducted most of the business of the empire. To appease the intellectuals who were severely critical of a woman assuming so much power, she encouraged learning and the literary and art world. Credit must be given to her for the blossoming of culture that contributed to the Tang dynasty's fame as the most brilliant epoch in Chinese history.

Over the years Wu Chao exercised more and more power, and in 674 she and her husband assumed the titles of Celestial Emperor and Celestial Empress, an almost sacred title which was calculated to distinguish them from all other rulers.

At the same time liberal decrees were issued to encourage industry and agriculture, to curtail excessive public spending, to lower taxes, and to reward officials who had given admirable service to the empire.

In 675 severe seizures weakened the Emperor. Unable to carry out government business he proposed that the Empress be made Regent. Strong opposition to his plan was voiced by the ministers and the proposal was withdrawn, but Wu Chao was little concerned since she was already active in affairs of state.

With the increasing weakness of the Emperor the matter of succession became urgent, particularly when the popular and able Crown Prince became suspiciously ill and died. Although no proof was forthcoming, poison was suspected since his popularity and ability stood in the way of Wu Chao's usurption of power when the Emperor died.

It became necessary to appoint a new Crown Prince and it fell to the next son, then about 21 years of age, to assume the title. But gossip was rife. The word was that the new Crown Prince was not Wu Chao's son, but rather the son of her sister. Considering the dates of the birth of Wu Chao's daughter and the subsequent birth of two more boys, it seemed most likely that the gossip had credence.

Meanwhile Wu Chao had been consulting a fortune teller who predicted that the Crown Prince was not suitable as a successor to the throne. Shortly afterwards the fortune teller was attacked and killed by bandits and investigations elicited the information that stores of arms were found in the Crown Prince's residence and one of his servants confessed to the crime committed on behalf of the Crown Prince. The Crown Prince was promptly exiled along with several of his friends, and the fourth child of Wu Chao was appointed to princedom.

The Emperor on his death bed produced a will entrusting the government to the President of the Chancellery and ordering the Crown Prince to refer all matters of serious consequence, both civil and military, to the Empress. Wu Chao, at 58 years of age, automatically became the Empress Dowager. But she was not satisfied with this role. However, the Prince proved so weak and incompetent that Wu Chao continued to exercise her authority.

She succeeded in deposing her son and was strongly supported by her courtiers and ministers. It was obvious that in spite of a society that maintained that rule by a woman was reprehensible, the officials considered that her efficient and orderly administration was acceptable. They did not trust the Crown Prince whose attempts to govern had proved weak and unpromising. Moreover he had indicated his unwillingness to leave decisions in Wu Chao's hands. The ministers decided "better the devil you know than the one you don't."

Wu Chao began to consolidate her power and remove any person likely to undermine her authority. The ex-Crown Prince was considered dangerous. A general was sent ostensibly to protect him, but so mistreated him that the young man committed suicide. He was then given posthumous recognition and his titles restored. A younger brother was installed as puppet emperor with Wu Chao as the recognized ruler.

Meanwhile the Crown Prince appointed by the deceased Emperor was languishing in exile and became the figurehead of a party of revolt. When Wu Chao decided to canonize her ancestors, a step that would bring her nearer to the throne, the opposition grew. Dissident factions united, a virulent document attacking the Empress was issued, and rebel forces began to grow. Knowing that the Empress intended to visit a nearby shrine, they plotted her arrest, but at the last minute heavy rains prevented her from making the journey. Open warfare broke out. A long and tedious campaign ensued, but in the end the government army was victorious and all officials who had supported the rebels or were suspected of connivance were exiled or put to death.

Wu Chao berated the Court for allowing opposition to reach the point of rebellion. She pointed out that the rebels had received little support from the people at large and that the army had remained loyal. She was now in a powerful position, believing that the nation as a whole stood by her, that the military and civil services for the most part supported her, and those officials who disliked her were in no position to mount opposition.

Emboldened by these assurances, Wu Chao decided to trample on convention and by skilful manipulation to establish herself as woman Emperor. Since she was already the real ruler it seemed to her that she should assume the title and end all pretence.

She began to choose talented men from the less privileged classes who had little opportunity to serve, but in this way she built for herself a devoted body of followers who knew their success and future depended entirely on her. Those who proved unable to carry out their responsibilities were subsequently punished or executed. Nor were her own relatives spared. Her two older brothers and their two sons were put to death, royal princes were forced to commit suicide, and as many as sixteen grandchildren were believed to have been killed, sometimes purportedly for gossiping about their grandmother.

A secret service was set up and on the strength of their reports, members of the imperial clan and officials and their families were exiled or wiped out. Nor were the upper class the only ones to feel her vengeance. Anyone who murmured a questionable thought or discussed the affairs of state in any way that appeared critical was reported by an informer and frequently suffered decapitation or strangulation. The purpose of these policies was, of course, to crush all opposition. A rebellion that occurred in 688, instigated by princes of the royal house ended in extermination of many of the imperial family.

To overcome the Confucian belief that women should not participate in the affairs of state, Wu Chao devoted herself to a form of Buddhism which acclaimed bodhisattvas, or disciples, who might be of either sex. She built numerous monasteries and promulgated through them the doctrines that supported her beliefs, taking to herself the title of "Holy Mother Divine Sovereign." She then deposed her son, the puppet governor, although it appears that she considered him to be her successor, and in October 690 she established an entire new dynasty known as the Chou. However, there is little to indicate that she intended to destroy the T'ang dynasty but regarded her rule as an aberration. But the puppet emperor was suspected by both the Wu clan and the supporters of the T'ang loyalists. His only son was nominally the Crown Prince, but his wife, the nominal Empress and his chief concubine, were accused of using sorcery to destroy Wu Chao and were summarily put to death.

Wu Chao, now 70 years of age, was concerned about the succession to the throne. Moreover, northern tribes were making advances on the kingdom and the T'ang armies and the Wu forces were attempting to repel the invasions. When the T'ang army proved successful, support grew for the T'angs, and the puppet Emperor was not looked upon with great favour. Demands were made that Chung Tsung, the Crown Prince, who had been banished, should be brought back as the heir apparent. In due course he did return to the palace since Empress Wu realised that after her death the T'ang dynasty would inevitably be restored.

According to accounts, which may be exaggerated by historians wishing to discredit Empress Wu, scandalous behaviour prevailed in the court. It is reported that Wu Chao established a male harem which was abhorred by her officials, but fear deterred them from protesting. Sure of her own power and authority she enjoyed the company of frivolous young favourites, particularly the Chang brothers who acquired considerable influence, but she was convinced that neither the Wu clan nor the T'ang supporters would dare to move against her. Banquets, gambling, drinking and festivities reportedly whiled away the nights. Flamboyant pageants and poems in praise of the beauty of the attendants were presented.

By the year 700 the Empress began to feel the weight of her years. She decided to spend some time in the country during the heat of the summer, particularly in the Shansi Mountains some distance from her capital in Loyang. By the following year her scandalous behaviour with the young men she had introduced to her court brought disgrace to her name. Advice from her ministers went unheeded and she herself became unpredictable. More and more support was turning to the T'angs.

About this time the Empress for some unexplained reason returned the Court to the old capital of Ch'ang-an where she remained for almost two years, removing once more to Loyang in the fall of 703. Here a serious case of trumped up charges by the Chang brothers against a loyal minister provoked serious repercussions. In the end Wu Chao stayed proceedings, but her prestige had been weakened by the very fact that she had entertained the possibility of the charges being true. Realizing the unpopularity of her young favourites, she attempted to appease her ministers by recalling some of the exiles and annulling charges and granting amnesty to the others who had suffered at her hands. However, serious charges were levelled against the Chang brothers who were called to account but were acquitted by the Empress. But matters did not rest there.

It was obvious that the Empress's health was declining and the Chang brothers schemed to find a way to survive the impending crisis. Had they been wise they would have aligned themselves with the Wu faction, but foolishly they antagonized both the Wu and the T'ang. A conspiracy to assassinate the brothers ended in their being trapped and beheaded one night in the palace by a force that included Crown Prince Chung Tsung and ministers of the government. When the Empress rose from her bed to discover the nature of the disturbance, the ministers demanded her abdication. Wu Chao returned to her room, making no comment. In the hours that followed, no one came to her support and the following day the Empress formally announced her abdication. Crown Prince Chung Tsung ascended the throne as Emperor and the T'ang dynasty was restored.

Wu Chao was given a palace on the outskirts of the city and was treated with respect by the new Emperor and his ministers. The name T'ang was restored to the imperial house, but the new Emperor, after years of exile and not in himself a strong leader, was ill-fitted to rule an empire. Moreover, his wife was a vicious and lewd woman on whom Chung Tsung depended. The Court found they had simply traded at least a capable if despotic mistress for a ruler with no ability to govern or control the Court. Before long he was replaced by one of Wu Chao's grandsons who became one of the most outstanding rulers of the famed T'ang dynasty. Known as the Brilliant Emperor, he reigned for half a century that is noted for its outstanding achievements and an outpouring of art and poetry.

In December 705, Wu Chao died at the age of 83. She had usurped a throne and established her own dynasty but in spite of her violent measures she had strengthened imperial rule and her expertise had saved the country from war and disintegration. As history assesses her contribution, the Chinese people admit, somewhat grudgingly, that she was a skilful and competent ruler, a unique and outstanding personage in their long history.

Chapter 5

A Kingdom Lost for a Concubine's Love
Yang Kuei Fei

Yang Kuei Fei
portrait courtesy of Li Xing Bai
leading contemporary painter

Thousands of tourists flock to Xian every year and after viewing the wonders of the terra cotta army that lay buried for nearly two thousand years, they visit the famous Hot Springs near by. But how many know the exotic scenes those hot springs witnessed or the powerful, history-making and often scandalous events that made life there the subject of national chronicles and folklore?

I wonder if they feel the ghosts of the past? Do they hear the sweet music of stringed instruments, the gentle songs of the beloved, or the plaintive laments of homesick concubines? Do they hear the gushing fountains, the splash of royalty bathing in the marble pools, the tread of endless lines of servants and eunuchs answering the bidding of their royal masters and mistresses. Do they smell the jasmine and roses, the incense of offerings, or see the dazzling display of fireworks and pageantry? Probably not.

Xian, once called Ch'ang-an, was the capital of China for fourteen dynasties and was one of the largest and most extravagant cities in the world.

Emperors built magnificent palaces and monuments to their own fame, the arts flourished, and travellers came from Europe in search of the riches of the exotic East.

In the year 718 AD as a meteor streaked across the sky, little Jade Ring was born to the wife of a petty provincial official named Yang in the province of Szechuan. The mother was frightened by the omen but the father insisted that it proved the girl would rise to great heights. But he was not to see the fulfilment of his expectations as he died when the child was quite young. The mother moved with her eight children to Ch'ang-an to take up residence with her husband's brother.

Uncle Yang never ceased to tell the children of the past history of the family and their links with nobility. For their own amusement Jade Ring and her three sisters would play-act stories of the queens and empresses, royal heroines and mythological princesses that they gathered from their uncle's tales. Always the stories were of great ladies, and their noble and royal themes shaped the thinking of the young girls and encouraged them to assume their place among the nobility.

Jade Ring was an acknowledged beauty, and added to her charm was her training in music and dance. She sang to her own accompaniment on the lute and was trained in dance by a famous actress of the time. Before long her beauty and accomplishments were known everywhere and came to the attention of the Emperor.

In 735 the Emperor, Ming Huang, was looking for a wife for one of his young sons and summoned Jade Ring to Court. Her sisters were ecstatic as they saw opportunities for their own advancement and a place in royal society. The prince was delighted with his young bride but the marriage was short-lived.

The Emperor who had proved himself an able administrator had brought peace and stability to the country. He was also a gifted musician, calligrapher and a patron of the arts. But when his favourite concubine died in childbirth, he fell into deep despair. He neglected his imperial duties, lost interest in life, and vented his grief on the Court. Powerful eunuchs took over government functions and the Royal Court was in disarray. It appeared that the Emperor, the Son of Heaven, was inconsolable.

To try and arouse the Emperor from his apathy, one of the courtiers suggested that the young prince's beautiful wife might be able to dispel the gloom that surrounded the Son of Heaven. As she was a talented musician and dancer, she was brought in to entertain the Emperor in an effort to rouse him from his melancholy mood. But Jade Ring had more daring aspirations. She longed to be the power behind the throne

When the Emperor saw her he was overwhelmed by her beauty and her charm, and immediately coveted her. But serious repercussions would doubtless ensue if he took her from his son. He, therefore, persuaded her to renounce her marriage vows and retire to a Taoist nunnery. Jade Ring was very depressed by the monastic life and felt that she had been abandoned, but before long she began to receive instructions from palace eunuchs on palace etiquette and the techniques of pleasing the Emperor. After a time she was brought back to the palace, and the Emperor enraptured by her charm and beauty gave her the name Kuei-fei, Precious Consort. In the meantime the Emperor had arranged for another wife for his son who still grieved for the wife he had lost to his father

More and more the Emperor lost interest in affairs of state. One poet of the period wrote a critical poem accusing the Emperor of not calling his court levees or attending to official business because of his obsession with his paramour. He noted that of the three thousand beautiful women in his harem, Kuei-fei was the only one he loved and she accompanied him on his journeys, joined him at his feasts and was his constant companion at night.

The Emperor and his Consort shared a love of music and both played instruments in the imperial orchestra. Kuei Fei was also a skilled dancer and singer and the Court became familiar with the nightly carousels of the seductive consort and her infatuated lover. Legend has it that one night in her dreams she was escorted by a moon maiden to the palace of the Goddess of the Moon where she heard the ethereal music of the Rainbow and Feathery Garment Dance. Returning to earth, Kuei Fei wrote the music for a new dance and the Emperor was so entranced with the script that he ordered his musicians to prepare it for presentation.

Yang Kuei Fei's position brought great benefits to her family. Her three sisters contracted convenient marriages that gave them entrance into noble society. They were given titles and received regular grants from the royal treasury to support their extravagant life styles. It was customary for them to scatter their largesse from their carriages as they rode through the countryside, dropping gold hairpins, jade brooches, embroidered slippers, or carved boxes for the less fortunate to pick up.

Other members of the family similarly benefited, a cousin rising to become Chief Minister wielding great power. Kuei Fei gave orders that were treated as imperial decrees, and her whims were satisfied at whatever cost. Her love of fresh lichee fruit caused relays of horses to be arranged to bring the fruit for her breakfast from Canton, more than 800 miles distant. The family's arrogance and the cost to the people for their upkeep created deep resentment throughout the realm. The poet Su Shi (1037-1101) expressed these feelings in a poem "A Lament for Lichees", in which he described the way in which the fruit was brought at great expense and hardship. He expressed pity for the men who were required to drive the carriages that covered hundreds of dusty miles or manned boats to cross the lakes in order to satisfy the whims of a court beauty.

With the arrival at Court of the Precious Consort and the Yang family, a change came over the Emperor. His reign had at the beginning shown great promise as he undertook administrative reforms and established libraries and schools. The empire was at peace and the arts flourished. There was an outpouring of music and poetry and the development of a wide range of examinations in classical studies. But unfortunately the Emperor's passion for his new concubine and the luxuries of the Court led him into self indulgence and extravagance that nearly brought the demise of the T'ang dynasty.

About this time there arrived in Ch'ang-an an officer from the northern frontier named An Lu-shan who had been defeated in battle and was to be court martialled. Fearing for his life he appealed on his knees with presents and tears of contrition to Chief Minister Yang, swearing to serve the Minister faithfully if his life was spared. Yang, having heard that An had knowledge of the northern barbarian languages and had military skills, considered that he might be used to stem the ever present danger of barbarian attacks and incursions into the realm. If he, Yang, could secure a reprieve for the prisoner, An would be eternally grateful and a useful pawn in the northern strategy. The Emperor listened to Yang's advice and An was reprieved and remained in the city. Before long this uncouth northerner managed to intrigue the court with his buffoonery and willingness to join in the bizarre court entertainment.

So popular did An become that he was accepted with delight by the ladies of the Court and was a welcome night time visitor, even with the Yang sisters and the Precious Consort herself. On one occasion when the Emperor was commenting on the unsurpassed beauty of Kuei Fei's breasts,

An added "and as smooth as satin to the touch." The courtiers present feared for An, but the Emperor was too engrossed in his favourite theme of the beauty of his beloved to notice the implication of An's comment.

Eventually An asked to be adopted by the Emperor and the Consort as their son, and at a grotesque ceremony to the merriment of the Court, he was granted his request. Soon afterwards An was sent north to consolidate the forces that were opposed to the northern intruders and while there he built up under his command a huge army of his tribesmen, purportedly to defend the empire against the aggressive barbarian intruders.

Meanwhile, at the famous hot springs near the city, the Emperor built palaces and baths where the Court indulged in their sensuous pleasures. Six marble pools were constructed in which the ladies of the Court might bathe, but the most sumptuous was the Emperor's. Here on moonlight nights he and his Precious Consort bathed together and the voluptuous figure of his concubine titillated her lover.

Kuei Fei's jealousy and temper were, however, sometimes more than the infatuated lover could bear. He became so angry with her on one occasion that he sent her back to her home, but so unbearable was his conduct without her that the palace was in turmoil. The Emperor refused to eat and lashed out at the eunuchs who tried to tempt him with food. In the opera The Palace of Eternal Youth, the Emperor cries out,

"How I long for her! Even if I had ambrosia
And heavenly elixirs, I should find them tasteless
Without the presence of the one I love,"

The chief eunuch begged the Emperor to ask Precious Consort to return. After various face-saving manoeuvres the remorseful Emperor finally sent a special chariot to bring his tearful and repentant paramour back to his loving embrace. In spite of the Emperor's assurance, Kwei Fei was always jealous of rivals, and her maids spied on Lady Plum Blossom, the Emperor's previous love for whom he still retained an affection.

When Kuei Fei discovered that the Emperor had truly spent a night with Lady Plum Blossom, she went to the Palace of Eternal Youth to pray for happiness. The occasion was the double seventh, the seventh day of the seventh month, when according to a famous legend the twin stars, the Heavenly Weaving Maid and Heavenly Cowherd, cross the Milky Way that separates them, and hold their yearly tryst. Although they are only permitted to meet once a year, their love is immortal, and they pity mortals because their love is so transient.

The Emperor discovered the Precious Consort at the Palace of Eternal Youth where incense rose, candles gleamed and flowers profusely decorated the hall. As Kuei Fei was praying the Emperor entered and asked what she was doing. She explained that she was praying for grace and skill, and he replied that she was more clever than any heavenly weaving maid who must wait a whole year before she could see her lover again. Kuei Fei pointed out that though they only met once a year, their love was eternal. Moved by her tears, the Emperor swore their love would never change. He burned incense and called the twin stars in heaven to witness their vow that they wished to be husband and wife and never be parted. After the death of the Emperor and Kuei Fei this story persisted and their love was immortalized in story and song.

Feasts and love intrigues continued within the Court and despite ominous warnings from the Chief Minister, the Emperor disregarded any accusations against his adopted son, An Lu-shan. But one day the sound of drums shook the palace walls and the Chief Minister hurried to inform the Emperor that An Lu-shan had revolted, his vast army had defeated the guards at a crucial pass and was advancing on the capital. The Emperor in distress ordered the princes and ministers to prepare to flee with him to Chengdu while the imperial generals recruited an army to defend the throne. He then ordered Kuei Fei to be called and told to be ready to leave at dawn.

Together with her sisters and other noble personages, Yang Kuei Fei joined the fugitives as they started out on the arduous journey to Chengdu. But the bodyguard accompanying the Emperor and his party were furious with Chief Minister Yang whom they blamed for the present debacle. When the party stopped for the night the troops mutinied. They turned on Yang and killed him, and their enmity towards the entire Yang family exploded. The Yang sisters were slain and then the soldiers demanded that the Precious Consort, Yan Kuei Fei, who had seduced the Emperor and drained the coffers of the empire, should suffer the same fate. The lovers were grief stricken. In desperation Kuei Fei asked that she might be sacrificed for the sake of the empire and the Emperor was forced to submit. Her dying wish was that she should commit suicide by strangulation in front of a Buddhist temple. Her wish was granted and the Emperor cried out in grief as the troops rejoiced at the destruction of the hated Yang clique.

When An Lu-shan was eventually assassinated by his son, the heir apparent usurped the throne. The Emperor, exhausted and tormented by remorse over the death of Kuei Fei, accepted the new ruler. Thus ended the longest and most brilliant T'ang reign, but did ensure the continuation of the dynasty. When the capital was recovered from the rebels, the old Emperor returned to Ch'ang-an where he was received with honour, and was allowed to live in one of his favourite palaces until he died in 761 at the age of 77.

Legend has it that he was tormented by the apparition of his lost love returning to remind him of their sworn promise of eternal love. A necromancer was called in to summon up the spirit of the Precious Consort and eventually the Emperor was able to learn from the Weaving Maid that Kuei Fei had become an immortal and was living in the fairy mountains beyond the oceans. The Emperor was comforted to know that he and Kuei Fei had previously been angels in heaven, had been sent to earth, but because of their faithfulness to each other they would return to heaven and be reunited.

The Nine Dragons Pool, Xi'An

Yuang Kuei Fei's mansion and the pool where she and the Emperor bathed.

Chapter 6

Superb Poetess
Li Ch'ing Chao

Li Ch'ing Chao

It was a soft spring day in the year 1097. A gentle breeze stirred the graceful willow boughs as they swayed lazily beside the Pure Jade Fountain.

Li Ch'ing Chao breathed a sigh of contentment as she watched the water spouts rise and fall in the crystal clear water of the fountain pool. Fish glistened in the blue waves, crimson flowers covered the water's banks, and blossoming pear and pomegranate trees added a fairyland quality to the scene. It was a peaceful vista, one of many in Jinan, city of seventy-two fountains.

From the folds of her dress Ch'ing Chao drew out a book and began to read. Her maidservant sat close by embroidering a delicate sash for her mistress. Before long the sun dipped behind the hills that surrounded the city and the two girls walked slowly back to their simple but comfortable three-roomed home. New thoughts were coursing through Ch'ing Chao's mind and forming phrases that had to be expressed in poetry.

Ch'ing Chao was a privileged girl who at fourteen years of age was uniquely endowed. Her father, a high official, was a well-known essayist, and her mother, coming from a family of scholars, was a writer of poetry and prose. Exposed to the joys of literature, Ch'ing Chao was encouraged by her parents to read, study and write. Not for her the old proverb "a woman's virtue lies in her ignorance." Her father gathered round him his literary friends whose open-mindedness encouraged their friend's unconventional daughter. Her parents did not subscribe to the widely held belief that a woman had no right to express her own thoughts or to enjoy freedom of action.

Obedience in childhood to father, in marriage to husband, and in widowhood to sons was the accepted code of the day. Women had, therefore, little opportunity to be creative contributors to society and were not normally prominent in literary or political circles. To write was considered immodest, and education contrary to tradition. But Ch'ing Chao's parents greeted her efforts with delight and encouraged her creativity. Her interest lay particularly in a poetic form known as tz'u, lyric verses sung to the well-known popular tunes of the Sung dynasty. Tz'u, as author Hu Ping-ching describes it, is a "fusion of scene and emotion." Because of Ch'ing Chao's intense delight in nature, the flowers, birds, trees, clouds, lakes and mountains were very much a part of her exquisite verse. In the following poem, translated by Kenneth Rexroth and Ling Chung, she eulogizes the cassia flowers, a composition to be sung to the tune Partridge Sky.

"Yellow bodies, light in colour and weight,
Gentle and soft in character.
Aloof, dispassionate,
Only their perfume is available.
They do not need bright green and red.
They are naturally the first choice of flowers.
The plum blossoms are jealous,
The chrysanthemums embarrassed.
In any exhibition of flowers.
They are the queens of mid-Autumn.
Other poets have been without taste
That they never wrote of them in the past." [1]

As Ch'ing Chao matured her poetry became more and more creative. Its sensuous quality, originality, lofty idealism, sensitivity to the world of nature and human experience expressed in simple language eventually earned for her the title of China's greatest poetess.

Nor was Ch'ing Chao gifted in poetry alone. Her creative genius found expression in prose, music and painting. As time passed, her deeply felt experiences of love, separation, war and loneliness added depth of womanly emotion in the lines that she penned.

Without a doubt her marriage added maturity and depth to her writing. At eighteen she married twenty-one year old Chao Ming-ch'eng, a student at the Imperial Academy, well known for his study of stone and bronze inscriptions and as a collector of ancient books and manuscripts. These two highly cultured young people were deeply in love and were of one mind in their interests and aspirations. They often tested each other's memory in recalling historical writings, or wrote poems replying to one another in identical rhythmic patterns.

Ch'ing Chao's poems of this early period of their married live are full of tenderness and charm. In a love poem sung to the tune of Song of Picking Mulberry, she reflects her radiant happiness.

"Evening comes with an onslaught of wind and rain,
washing clean the heat and glare.
I put away my reed pipes,
face the flower-formed mirror, applying light make-up.
Red silk gauze so sheer my white skin shines through,
snowy-smooth, cream fragrance.
I smile and say to my husband
Tonight inside the light curtains, pillow and mat will be cool." [2]

Poems like this shocked the feudal literary circles. Whilst acknowledging that Li Ch'ing Chao was one of the best writers of tz'u poetry, one critic spoke of her licentious language and deplored that a learned woman of an official family would be so unscrupulous.

For ten years Ch'ing Chao and her husband worked together, supporting themselves on the meagre salary that Ming-ch'eng received as a local magistrate. They lived frugally, spending their money on books and reproductions of inscriptions, rare paintings and antique ritual vases, incense burners, pots and goblets, sometimes pawning personal items to pay for the coveted treasures. Borrowing rare books from friends and relatives, they laboriously copied them to add to their collection. During these ten years they collected and catalogued, carefully examined antiques, studied inscriptions that gave much information relative to ancient social and political institutions, and they built large cabinets to house their precious collection.

Because of the nature of his work, Ming-ch'eng was frequently away from home, and left alone, Ch'ing Chao expressed her longing for him in some of her very beautiful poems.

> Deep in the silent inner room
> Every fibre of my soft heart
> Turns to a thousand strands of sorrow
> I loved the Spring
> But the Spring is gone.
> As rain hastens the falling petals,
> I lean on the balustrade,
> Moving from one end to the other.
> My emotions are still disordered.
> Where is he?
> Withered grass stretches to the horizon
> And hides from sight
> Any road by which he might return. [3]

In 1126 as the Sung dynasty began to weaken, Ch'ing Chao was very concerned about the future of her country and her people, and the couple were worried about the security of their precious collection. Early the following year Ming-cheng's mother died and he left for the city of Nanking to attend her funeral. Fearing for the safety of his acquisitions he took with him fifteen cartloads of books, but was forced to leave behind the heavy tomes, the ancient bronzes, and paintings.

The corruptness of the dynasty led a neighbouring state to take aggressive steps and shortly after Ming-cheng's departure the northern Chin seized the Sung capital. The Sung Emperor failed to resist and fled to an area south of the Yangtze River where he established a southern Sung dynasty with the capital in Hangzhou. Ch'ing Chao was extremely perturbed by the corruption and incompetence of the court and she condemned the rulers for their non-resistance to the enemy. When the invaders reached the city where Ch'ing Chao was alone at the time, ten rooms of the couple's books were burned to ashes.

In 1128, to escape the devastation caused by the invasion, Ch'ing Chao fled south crossing the Huai River to join her husband. This journey marked a turning point in her life. She ventured into political satire and her poem, "A Satire on the Lords Who Crossed the Yangtze in Flight from the Chin Troops" made her popular with the people but angered many powerful officials.

Ming-cheng was able to provide a comfortable life for the couple with his appointment as a magistrate, but unfortunately the following year he fell fatally ill and died at the age of forty-nine.

Far away from home and country, trying to protect the precious collection they had managed to save, and mourning her beloved, Ch'ing Chao suffered almost unbearable loneliness.

> The River of heaven turns across the sky.
> All the world is covered with bed curtains.
> It grows cold.
> Tear stains spread on my mat and pillow.
> I get up and take off my clothes
> And listlessly ask "How late at night is it?"
> The green feather pattern of lotus pods,
> The gold thread design of lotus leaves,
> Seem small and sparse on my gauze sleeping robe.
> The same weather as in the old days,
> The same dress I wore then
> Only my arms are empty of love,
> And our past is gone forever. [4]

These lines not only expressed Ch'ing Chao's grief but that of the many who had lost their homes and fled to the inhospitable south. Life remained unsettled as the enemy advanced and the Court continued to flee. In the course of her enforced flight she lost almost all her prized collection, some stolen, some abandoned and some donated to the Court.

In 1132 when she was forty-nine and living in the new capital in the Southern Sung Court, events took a strange turn. According to unverified sources she married an official but became a victim of abuse and divorced him shortly afterwards, accusing him also of misappropriation of government funds. He was convicted but she was imprisoned for a time for bringing a lawsuit against her husband. Attempts by later scholars to refute these stories, possibly to clear the name of the great poetess, have left this period of her life in shadow. Some claimed that the official she offended with her poetry fabricated the story, but it may be that beset by loneliness and the chaotic conditions of the period, she did seek to find some stability in a marriage.

In spite of all her hardships, however, she continued to find solace in poetry and to celebrate in imagery and symbolism the beauty of the world around her. She branched out from her tz'u style of poetry to write what was known as shih, a type of more formal regular verse, but her fame rests on her lyric qualities best expressed in tz'u.

Very little is known about her later years. She may have stayed with the family of her younger brother but was forced again to move because of the threat of war. She died at the age of sixty-eight, the author of many hundreds of poems of which only fifty have survived in a volume entitled *Tz'u of Pure Jade*. But her fame during her life time and the acknowledged beauty and sensitivity of her work that has survived, have won for her the unchallenged title of China's Greatest Poetess. Her own lines written of another, are a fitting tribute to this outstanding woman,

"What need is there of petals azure or pink,
When she herself is the fairest flower of all!"

Chapter 7

The Power Behind The Throne
T'zu-Hsi's Rise to Power (Part 1)

An Empress Doll circa 1900

In 1644 China was conquered by the Manchus and the rule of the Ching Dynasty was established. The Han people, the vast majority of China, considered the Manchus as outsiders, foreigners, and usurpers. Although the dynasty lasted until 1911, the Manchus were never accepted as legitimate rulers.

In the Manchu hierarchy certain clans were exceedingly powerful and were given special privileges. From the Yehonala clan came many of the wives and concubines of the emperors.

On November 3, 1835 a baby girl named Orchid was born into the family of an obscure official in Anhui province. Her father died when she was about three years of age, and her mother decided to move to Peking with Orchid and a baby sister to live with rich and influential relatives. Travelling by barge they made the pleasant trip on the Grand Canal and eventually arrived at their new home on Pewter Lane in what was known as the Tartar section of the capital city.

Because the family belonged to the Yehonala clan, Orchid became known as Yehonala, a name that remained permanently hers. Life was pleasant in Pewter Lane. One-storey houses with curved roofs and ornamental tiles were built around courtyards featuring lotus ponds and flowering shrubs. Yehonala, curious and quick-witted, was always eager to explore her surroundings and to watch the wedding and funeral processions that passed her gate, or the caravans carrying pewter wares from Yunnan to the stores on her street that featured these favoured wares. Without questioning she would accompany one of the household staff to the markets nearby, listen to the story-tellers or watch the puppet shows, and examine all the clothes and trinkets for sale at the stalls. But the most fun was to be had in company with her cousin Jung Lu when they played together in the neighbourhood.

"Let's sail boats on the Jade Canal," Jung Lu suggested as he picked up a likely looking twig.

"Mine will beat yours," Yehonala replied as she chose a sturdy sample.

Throwing their 'boats' into the canal they watched as the twigs drifted slowly. But a passing sampan stirred the water and Jung Lu's twig ended on a sand bar while Yehonala's was caught in the vortex of a small whirlpool and then was thrust into the current, carrying it far down the canal.

"Well tomorrow I'll bring my eagle kite and fly it in the fields," boasted Jung Lu.

Not to be outdone, Yehonala said, "I can recite from the Book of the Three Characters."

"But I can say the twenty-five rules of filial piety," countered Jung Lu.

"I'm learning those too," persisted Yehonala as they made their way home.

"Be careful," Jung Lu shouted as he and Yehonala flattened themselves against a brick wall. A royal person was being borne on a palanquin and the bearers were jostling pedestrians out of the way. Then came a line of carts piled high with goods and the children waited for them to pass. Yehonala was learning about life in her city.

As the two children grew, Jung Lu came to admire his cousin and they fell deeply in love with one another. Yehonala at 16 years of age had become a charming young woman who fascinated those with whom she came in contact. She had been trained in all the arts considered suitable for daughters of good families, embroidery, painting and music. But the young couple were never to realize their dreams.

Emperor Hsien-feng had lost his wife who had been childless, and after a twenty-seven month period of mourning, sixty of the most beautiful

Manchu girls were summoned to the court in the Forbidden City to be selected as consorts and concubines for the Emperor. When the number had been pared down, sixteen young women were summoned to the palace to be presented to the Empress Dowager and her son, the young Emperor. Among them were Sakota, phlegmatic sister of the dead empress, and Yehonala, charming, gifted and with overwhelming ambition.

To the Empress Dowager fell the task of assigning the young women to their status groups. Not considering any of them worthy to be placed in the first rank, the Dowager Empress assigned Sakota to the second class and Yehonala to the third. However, Yehonala, taking great pains to ingratiate herself into the good graces of the Empress Dowager, eventually won her approval and became known as the Yi Concubine. The Emperor himself had been fascinated by Yehonala and passing by one of the pavilions housing the concubines, he heard a sweet voice singing. On inquiry he discovered the singer to be the girl that had attracted him at their first meeting. He promptly ordered the eunuch to bring her to his room that night.

Outside the Emperor's apartment was an ivory table on which were tablets of jade engraved with the names of the concubines. On retiring the Emperor would turn over the tablet of the one whom he favoured and a eunuch would carry the chosen one, enveloped in silk, and lay her naked at the foot of the Emperor's bed. So enamoured was the Emperor of Yehonala that her tablet was consistently overturned.

Sakota finally became recognized as the Emperor's consort and bore him a girl child who died soon after birth. Yehonala, on the other hand, bore a healthy boy in April 1856, and she was thereupon raised to the rank of first class. Her enemies scurrilously suggested that the weakly, unpopular emperor was incapable of fathering a child and that Jung Lu, now an officer in the Imperial Guard, was Yehonala's lover and father of the child. But the powerful eunuchs who controlled the destiny of the royal family, had been so wooed by Yehonala with her gifts and charm that no indication of any irregularity was seriously considered or proved.

Yehonala was a vivacious conversationalist and her gracious manner, pleasant voice and sparkling eyes gave her a magnetic quality that mesmerized her listeners, although her enemies found to their dismay that those same eyes could flash with anger and the smooth tongue had a cutting edge. It is questionable that Yehonala was literate when she first arrived at the Forbidden City. Reading and writing were not included in the education of Manchu girls, but with the help of the chief eunuch and factions within the palace who were vying for ascendancy, she was able to express her wishes. As time went by she acquired literary skills so that in later years she was able to read all the documents that came into her hands and write the many edicts and memorials that appeared over her signature.

At this time a rebellion in the south, known as the Taiping Uprising, spread with such success that by 1853 the rebels had swept through province after province and had captured Nanking, the second most important city in the realm. Yehonala, irked by the ineffective resistance of the imperial troops, persuaded the Emperor to appoint a Chinese general whom she considered superior to the Manchu officers. When the outcome of the campaign was favourable to the imperial forces and the insurrection was finally suppressed, it was considered a good omen and Yehonala basked in the light of this success.

Meanwhile new problems were arising on the international level. The Celestial Emperor considered foreign emissaries as mere bearers of tribute from lesser kings, an attitude that enraged foreign envoys. After the Opium War (1839-1842) when Britain had successfully forced China to open her ports to extensive trade, including the nefarious importation of opium, relations had been strained. British subjects had been granted extraterritoriality in cities such as Shanghai so that they no longer came under Chinese law. Hong Kong had been ceded to Britain, and a huge indemnity had been extracted.

In 1856 an incident in Canton further exacerbated the situation and Yehonala, twenty-one years of age, unschooled in international affairs, urged the Emperor to order the High Commissioner in Canton to reject negotiations. The Imperial Court then refused to abide by the treaties which they claimed had been signed under duress, whereupon British and French forces were dispatched to enforce implementation of the terms.

The Emperor published an edict at Yehonala's urging, denouncing the western barbarians and offering to let them trade with the Celestial Kingdom if they were prepared to pledge allegiance to the Son of Heaven. The European leaders were scandalized by this shocking pronouncement and when their envoys were seized and tortured the foreign powers immediately advanced on Peking.

Yehonala maintained that the army was capable of withstanding the foreign onslaught but the Emperor decided to flee the capital. Although the Court was then in residence at the Summer Palace some distance from the centre of the city, the Emperor and his advisers decided to leave. In this he was encouraged by Su Shan, a powerful official whom he unwittingly trusted. After appointing his brother, Prince Kung, as Plenipotentiary, the Emperor issued a decree that the war should continue at all costs. The weak and vacillating Son of Heaven ignored the Yi Concubine's plea that he should offer large rewards for the killing of the invading barbarians and should himself stay and face the invaders. But accompanied by some Manchu princes, the two Empresses Sakota and Yehonala, the young heir apparent, faithful eunuchs and Court officials, the Emperor left in confusion for Jehol, north of the Great Wall. Accompanying the royal party was a strong detachment of troops including Yehonala's cousin, Jung Lu. On the three day journey over mountainous roads Yehonala considered her position and began to fear that her hold on the Emperor was waning.

With the advance of the allied troops, Prince Kung realized that the only chance the Chinese government had for survival was in capitulation. Ignoring the Emperor's edict he submitted to the invading forces and signed a treaty. But the British and French troops looted and ransacked the magnificent Summer Palace and eventually burned it to the ground. Yehonala's favourite residence was utterly destroyed and its treasures removed to foreign lands.

Once Yehonala was out of the way and the Emperor in such poor health that he was unlikely to survive his return to Peking, the Princes Yi and Chang and the corrupt Su Shun plotted to set up a regency. When the Emperor finally succumbed to his illness, Su Shun urged his conspirators to have Yehonala killed but they feared the vengeance of the Yehonala clan. The Yi concubine was in mortal danger but with great astuteness she planned to forestall any attempts on her life. With extreme composure and gentleness she posed as the innocent young widow and carefully avoided any contact with Jung Lu that would cause gossip. Through the chief eunuch who was devoted to her, she, with the support of Empress Sakota, sent a message to Prince Kung in Peking advising him of a conspiracy against the imperial family.

When news of the Emperor's death reached Peking and the Edict from the three self-appointed regents was issued, there were widespread protests. Word was sent to the little Emperor in Jehol urging him to appoint the two Empresses as co-Regents. As the deceased Emperor's body was being prepared for the journey to the capital, tension was mounting in Jehol. The journey would be long and tedious. The coffin, placed on an enormous covered platform and surrounded by satin and gold curtains, would be carried shoulder high by bearers in rhythmic steps over the one hundred and fifty miles to the capital. Regents and high officials were obliged to accompany the procession, while the two Dowager Empresses could travel quickly to Peking to be in readiness to receive the cortege when it arrived.

Jung Lu and the Yehonala troops were ordered to accompany the Emperor's remains. Prince Yi's troops were detailed to escort the Empresses. Plans had been laid by the three self-appointed regents for Yehonala to be assassinated as she rode through a mountain pass. But Jung Lu discovered the plan and when the royal bier was laid down for the night and all mourners knelt in respect, legend has it that Jung Lu and his loyal clansmen leapt to their horses and without fear of pursuit dashed to the defence of his beloved. Whatever the explanation, Yehonala arrived safely in Peking and prepared to receive the funeral procession

Ever mindful of the respect owed to the dead Emperor, Yehonala postponed all reprisals and courteously carried on with the formal rites and ceremonies, greeting the cortege at the city gates with suitable pomp and reverence. The little six year old Emperor with the Co-Empresses at his side, thanked the gathered assembly for bearing his father's remains to his final resting place.

Su Shun was consumed with bitterness and railed at the two princes for neglecting to do away with the Yi Concubine long ago. The self-appointed Regents ordered Yehonala to leave the palace and issued an edict announcing themselves as the sole authorities appointed by the late Emperor. But the edict lacked one essential requirement, the official imperial seal. They were unable to affix it to the document because Yehonala, probably with the help of her devoted eunuch, had managed to expropriate it. Prince Kung immediately issued an edict, stamped with the official seal, naming the two Empresses as Co-Regents, and ordered the arrest of the three conspirators. Su Shun was beheaded, his enormous fortune expropriated by Yehonala, and the two princes were stripped of their rank and sent silken cords, the traditional command to commit suicide.

As soon as the Empresses were confirmed as co-regents they issued a proclamation stating that they were willing to take over the heavy responsibilities thrust upon them. Simultaneous they issued new titles for the boy Emperor and for themselves. Sakota became Tz'u An (motherly and restful) and Yehonala Tz'u Hsi (motherly and auspicious).

Prince Kung's support of the Empresses was an unwilling alliance that had been based on his loathing for Su Shun and the bitter emnity between himself and his cousin Prince Yi. With these enemies out of the way, Prince Kung became overconfident, assuming powers and acting in ways that Yehonala considered disrespectful. Finally during an audience with Tz'u Hsi his behaviour broke protocol and he was stripped of his official powers. But the Manchu princes were not yet ready to accept Tz'u Hsi's supremacy. Prince Kung, having learned his lesson, was therefore graciously re-instated by the Empress.

Prince Kung had agreed to the harsh terms of the Western Powers, knowing that the Taiping Rebellion was not completely stamped out. But foreign aggression continued unabated. Considering China to be defenseless, Russia, Japan and finally Germany joined France and Britain in annexing territory, occupying desirable areas and demanding huge indemnities for any infraction of treaty terms.

Tz'u Hsi's total lack of knowledge of western ways caused endless problems. Chinese protocol demanded that all persons accorded the rare privilege of audience with the royal court were required to kowtow, kneeling in obeisance to the Emperor and Empress. Foreign envoys refused to perform this act of subservience and eventually Tz'u Hsi benevolently excused them because as barbarians they were incapable of appreciating civilized customs. Another source of great irritation was the missionary movement that saw large numbers of "foreign devils" intruding on China's beliefs and way of life.

"Ladies of the Court", period dress

Between the years of 1896 and 1899 China was divided up by the imperialist powers into spheres of influence where the imperialists exercised controls and took over important aspects of government. Foreign countries leased rights to anchor their warships in all major ports, and the rights to construct railways and open mines were being taken over by foreign governments. Taiwan, since ancient times a part of China, was ceded under pressure to Japan, and Hong Kong had been ceded to Britain who also acquired rights on the adjacent mainland known as Kowloon. Huge indemnities were negotiated which meant that China had to borrow from foreign countries, thus increasing her reliance on the imperialist powers, and had to accept imperialist development of economic development.

Russia, Britain, Germany, France, the U.S., Japan, and to a lesser extent, Italy and Austria were all engaged in pressuring China and demanding rights and privileges. Concessions were established where the laws and rules of the imperialist powers were adopted and Chinese citizens were forbidden to enter without permission. The waterfront section of the Bund in Shanghai had a sign "No Chinese or dogs allowed".

Chapter 8

Tz'u Hsi as Regent (Part 2)

Tz'u Hsi, like all China's rulers, was heavily dependent on the eunuchs for all her information and needs. Eunuchs, although despised by other men and the populace in general, nevertheless had during the centuries acquired enormous power. Guardians of the harem, the source of information from the outside world, controllers of all goods and services entering the palace, placed enormous power in their hands. Throughout history head eunuchs had sometimes become more powerful than the emperor himself, and many eunuchs were able to amass vast fortunes on commissions and bribes.

Lavish expenditures of the Court were encouraged by the eunuchs who made money on every transaction, tripling and quadrupling the cost of all items. Tz'u Hsi, for instance, was fond of jewellery which was kept in 600 boxes in a room especially set aside for this purpose. Pearls and jade were her favourite jewels. Strings of pearls hung from her head-dress, a cape of pearls was often fitted over her shoulders, rings and ornaments of the best jade adorned her person, and coral, gold and ivory decorated her belongings. She ordinarily had about three hundred dresses mostly in rich brocades or embroidered satins, the embroidery for one dress sometimes taking a skilled artisan a year to complete. She was also passionately fond of the theatre, arranging for theatrical companies to stage elaborate plays or sometimes acting herself, usually appearing as a goddess or royal personage. The cost of this luxurious living placed a heavy burden on the people and led to bribery and corruption beyond belief.

The eunuch An-te-hai had been a vital force in Tz'u Hsi's rise to power. When she first arrived at Court she shrewdly realized the importance of winning the favour of this Chief Eunuch. In her inimitable way she cunningly flattered and encouraged him and always rewarded his faithful service with marked generosity. It is probable that he arranged for the Emperor to stroll in the garden when she was singing so that his attention was drawn to her. He is considered by some to have acted as an intermediary between her and Jung Lu when, according to some reports, they carried on an illicit love affair. Tz'u Hsi depended on him to carry messages, including the sending of the dispatch to Prince Kung from Jehol to warn him of the conspiracy.

One fatal mistake that An-te-hai made was to trust so securely in the favour of Tz'u Hsi that he failed to pay due respect to the other Empress, Tz'i An. Although she was not much involved in affairs of state, she resented the Chief Eunuch's neglect of her. On another occasion the eunuch had, in the opinion of Prince Kung, insulted him and the Prince never forgot a discourtesy. This unbecoming conduct cost the eunuch his life.

Manchu laws forbade palace eunuchs to leave the palace unless accompanying the Empresses. An-te-hai in the summer of 1869, with the consent of Tz'u Hsi, journeyed to Shandong province to collect tribute. The Governor, angered at An-te-hai's visit in royal style and the exorbitant demands made on him, complained to Prince Kung. The Prince took the information not to Tz'u Hsi but to Tz'u An whom he persuaded somewhat fearfully to issue a decree for the decapitation of the pompous eunuch. The Governor received the decree, invited the eunuch to his mansion and promptly carried out the execution. Tz'u Hsi knew nothing of the death of her favourite eunuch until news reached the capital and her fury was vented on the terror-stricken Tz'u-An. The gulf between the two Empresses widened and Prince Kung was discarded as a counsellor in favour of other officials more favourable to Tz'u Hsi

The new chief eunuch, Li Lien-ying, had helped nurse the dying Emperor in Jehol and may have been responsible for the furtive removal of the State Seal, which was turned over to Yehonala. He was unfailingly faithful to her when she became co-regent, and obeyed only her orders. He served her with due deference, but behind his manner lay an iron will. As the royal family were cut off from all contact with their subjects to the point where streets were cleared, shops closed and even palace workers disappeared when royalty approached, the eunuchs were the royal families only touch with reality. Li was unscrupulous, greedy and cruel but his pleasant voice and gentle behaviour in the presence of his mistress gave no evidence of the dangers that surrounded the throne.

Tz'u Hsi's son, the boy Emperor T'ung Chih, suffered from the same isolation as his mother. The Emperor was not physically strong and his health was further impaired by his dissipation outside the walls of the palace. Aided by his eunuch, he would escape by a small private door in the outer wall and incognito spend his nights in opium dens, gaming houses and brothels. His behaviour was not unknown to the Chief Eunuch, Li Lien-ying who without doubt secretly encouraged his vices. Nor was Tz'u Hsi guiltless. She was certainly aware of the Emperor's vices but was unable to do anything to prevent his excesses that would inevitably lead to his early demise.

In March 1872 the two Empresses, guided by the Clan Council, announced that a bride had been selected for the Emperor. She was 15-year old A-lu-te, who had both royal Manchu blood and Mongol ancestors, and, therefore, considered a binding force in the Manchu Mongol alliance. But the innocent young bride was ill prepared to face the bisexual, syphilitic T'ung Chih. Quarrels were frequent both between the young couple and between the Emperor and his advisers and his two imperial mothers

A date for the young Emperor's accession to the throne was fixed for February 1873, and it was hoped that the new responsibilities would encourage him to rectify his behaviour and give attention to matters of state. But the Emperor was in no mood to change his ways. In anger at criticism he fired his entire cabinet, at the same time alienating the Grand Council, the Clan Council, officials, princes and governors.

The two Empress Dowagers were asked to intervene in the belief that they had some control over the willful young man, but before long the Emperor paid the price of his licentiousness. The end was not long in coming. It was announced that he had contracted smallpox, an affliction often associated with syphilis. The two Dowager Empresses, expressing deep concern for his well being, stated that they would willingly handle matters of State during his illness. But the young Emperor died on January 13, 1875, and the immediate question was, who would succeed him?

The Emperor had not designated a successor before he died. The young Empress was pregnant and should she have a son he would be the rightful heir. But Tz'u Hsi did not wish to wait for such an event. There were three contenders Prince Kung's 17-year old son, or one of the sons of two other Manchu princes. Tz'u Hsi knew that her position was in jeopardy if the 17-year old came to the throne as he would assume power almost immediately and her regency would end. Also, Kung's son and one of the other contenders were of the same generation as the deceased emperor and were, therefore, disqualified from rendering ancestral worship, which meant the tragic situation of the Emperor going into the spirit world without support.

As the Emperor had not given any instructions regarding his successor, the matter had to be finally decided by the Grand Council. Tz'u Hsi was determined to sway the Council to her choice, namely the four-year old son of her sister who was married to one of the Manchu princes. Arguments and counter arguments raged back and forth as the princes and councillors supported and countered the various proposals. The suggestion was made that the decision be delayed until A-lu-te's child was born, but Tz'u Hsi craftily warned that the Taiping rebels were still active and that a vacant throne would simply invite another uprising. When the matter came to a vote, the princes voted to uphold the claims of two of the prince's sons, but the ministers and councillors supported Tz'u Hsi. Victory went to Tz'u Hsi by a vote of fifteen to ten.

To crown her victory the Empress sent for the child to be brought to the palace immediately regardless of the fact that there was a howling dust storm sweeping the city, hardly an auspicious omen. A palanquin was sent to the child's home. The little boy was awakened from his sleep, wrapped in silk quilts, and carried to the palace where he was taken to kowtow to the body of the dead Emperor who lay clothed in his sumptuous burial garments. The child was terrified by the eerie light, the weeping widow kneeling at the bier, the angry princes, the ornately dressed ministers and the wily eunuch Li and his henchmen.

When Tz'u Hsi announced the decision of the Council there was a public outcry. Laws of decendancy had been violated. The deceased Emperor's soul was in limbo without the comfort and support of the required ancestor worship. Meanwhile A-lu-te pined in despair and within a few days she was dead. Suicide? Foul play? No one knew but there were hints of poison.

Tz'u Hsi set to work to consolidate her position, ridding herself of former officials including Prince Kung and other members of the Council who had opposed her. Shortly after A-lu-te's death, Tz'u Hsi herself fell ill, a questionable coincidence that seemed to indicate a desire on someone's part to purge the Court of all those associated with the deceased Emperor. Tz'u Hsi, however, recovered although she remained in poor health for several years. Despite her illness her enemies laid the blame for A-lu-te's death and the countless ills that befell the empire on her, attempting to build up her reputation as a malicious, power-seeking monster.

Although she held sway, Tz'u Hsi was not free of criticism. The Censors, a Board appointed to keep watch over the Court, frequently sent written epistles known as memorials to the Dowager Empress pointing out the extravagance and corruption of the Court. Tz'u Hsi acknowledged the memorials but ignored the criticism.

The other source of opposition to her conduct of affairs was Prince Kung. She was determined to rid herself of this thorn in the flesh. As evidence of her enormous power she was able in 1884 to issue a decree stating that since Prince Kung had exceeded his rights, was guilty of nepotism and self-aggrandisement, and rumour had suggested that he was guilty of treason, he must suffer the consequences. However, she expressed a wish not to be overly harsh and, therefore, allowed him to retain his Princedom and its benefits, but relieved him of his offices and duties so that he might retire into private life and take greater care of his health.

To the delight of the eunuch Li Lien-ying, the decree was read from the throne in the audience chamber. Gone were the days when the Empress hid behind a yellow curtain. Now she sat in all her splendour on the Peacock Throne, looking down on the men who seemed powerless to oppose her. Prince Kung went into retirement and remained in seclusion for ten years until events brought him again to the fore.

The new Emperor, Kuang Hsu, was only four years old when he came in 1875 to live with his official mother, Tz'u An, and his aunt Tz'u Hsi. His early days had not been happy ones. His mother was a sadistic woman, a child beater, who locked her children in closets for punishment and caused the death of four of her children from malnutrition and abuse. It was not surprising, therefore, that the little Emperor, the sole survivor of this unhappy household, was a nervous, stuttering child when he arrived at the palace. To add to his problems, his palace tutor rigidly schooled him in the most restrictive Confucian etiquette and taught utter submission to the two Empresses as an antidote to the disreputable behaviour of the previous Emperor.

Tz'u Hsi was not well enough until the boy was nine to take much part in his upbringing. Any misbehaviour on the boy's part was met with frightening isolation or severe punishment that terrorized him. With long hours of study and practice in official ceremonies, a frugal diet, often tormented by malicious eunuchs, Kuang Hsu had little opportunity to grow into a balanced, stable ruler. A permanent dislike of servants and particularly eunuchs, led him as an adult to be sensitive to the slightest discourtesy and to order the punishment of offenders. The result was that in the teahouses malicious gossip was spread that reached the outside world that had no access to the Court. As a teen Kuang Hsu showed no desire for the frivolous escapades of the former Emperor. Rather he tended at times to withdraw into an almost ascetic life style, eating alone and becoming almost a prisoner in the restricted world in which he found himself.

In 1881 Tz'u An who had had no previous illness suddenly collapsed and the following day died at the age of forty-four. As usual, gossip immediately conjured up intrigue and murder, laid of course at Tz'u Hsi's door, but recent speculation suggests that she died of a viral flu.

Tz'u Hsi, still not in the best of health, was now the sole Dowager Empress and Regent with full responsibility for the imperial family and the maintaining of peace among the various rival elements of the Court. Appeals were made to her for approval and her decisions became significant. Kuang Hau was only nine and to the outside world Tz'u Hsi became the ruler of China. But the power struggle between reactionaries and reformers was still a major concern and the Empress Dowager was caught in the tussle.

When the Emperor was eleven Tz'u Hsi announced his engagement to his cousin of the Yehonala clan, thus strengthening the clan's hold on power. In 1887 the Emperor, at seventeen, came of age but did not assume power for two years. Meanwhile the girl had developed into a fine-looking, charming person but after a lavish marriage ceremony in 1889 it proved to be a very unhappy union. Quarrels broke out frequently and the Emperor made it clear that he disliked the wife who had been chosen for him. In all probability Tz'u Hsi had purposely chosen a woman willing to report to her on the Emperor's doings. Two concubines were also chosen for him and were regarded with jealousy by his wife. But when the Emperor became ill, doctors indicated that he was not physically able to father children, and the unstable empire was left with no promise of an heir.

Tz'u Hsi, age fifty-four, was now compelled by the Emperor's marriage and ascent to the throne, to relinquish her regency. She retired to her favourite residence, the restored Summer Palace, where she spent enormous sums beautifying the vast grounds and actually appropriated Navy funds to build herself a beautiful marble boat that is still a show piece. She gloried in the beautiful landscape, the hills, the flowers and streams, the canals and marble bridges, and the exquisite halls and gateways that adorned the palace grounds. Attended by eunuchs and ladies-in-waiting she drifted on the waters of the man-made lake or listened to the songs, the flutes and the poems offered by her attendants.

But Tz'u Hsi was by age and rank still senior to the Emperor. Through her loyal eunuch, Li Lien-ying, she ordered appointments and dismissals, and by sheer will power continued to keep control of affairs of state. She also acquired from the eunuch Li the affectionate title of Old Buddha when her prayers for rain during a severe drought were answered. The name soon became known throughout the country, and in a land where 'old' is synonymous with wise and venerable, the Empress was exceedingly pleased with the title.

In her new residence the Empress took a keen interest in the gardens, knew the names of all the varieties of flowers, and used flowers profusely in the many festivals associated with the seasons. Her interest in theatricals continued, and to this day the stage in the Summer Palace is very much in evidence, with its balcony for musicians and the platform where the Empress and her Court sat to view the performances.

But walks, picnics, festivals and theatricals, supervision of her private silk and embroidery industries, and constantly surrounded day and night by ladies-in-waiting, eunuchs and military guards, did not make up to Tz'u Hsi for the loss of her supreme position. However, in 1894 she was to celebrate her sixtieth birthday which, according to Chinese tradition, called for a monumental celebration. Provincial governors and officials throughout the empire were honoured with invitations, the cost of the festivities to be borne as a birthday gift by contributions of one quarter of the official's salary for the year. Triumphal arches were to be built over the whole five miles of road leading from the Forbidden City to the Summer Palace, and along which endless processions would wind their way bearing precious treasures of jewels, carvings, furniture, porcelain, carpets, silks and embroideries. The old Buddha was in her element preparing for this joyous occasion.

Fate, however, decreed otherwise. Korea, always considered to be under the protection of the Celestial Kingdom, was coming increasingly under the influence of Japan. In 1894 war broke out with Japan. Corruption and grossly inept operations led to the ignominious defeat of the Chinese forces. Reluctantly Tz'u Hisi announced that she could not enjoy the planned festivities in the face of her country's humiliation. The fact that she had drained the Navy of its funds and had thereby undermined its effectiveness was not revealed. In order to lay the blame somewhere, Tz'u Hsi reproached the Emperor for allowing his forces to enter upon such a disastrous war, a charge which brought further estrangement between the Dowager and the Emperor, led to factional strife within the palace, and was exacerbate by the death of the Emperor's mother, Tz'u Hsi's sister. Outwardly, however, relations appeared cordial, and the Emperor made his customary filial calls upon the Dowager, ostensibly to discuss matters of State.

In the summer of 1898, however, the Emperor embarked on a policy that shook the empire. Party strife within the Forbidden City and in government circles had become intense. Radical progressives particularly from the South were urging reforms but were strongly opposed by the reactionaries within the Court. In April 1898 Prince Kung, who might have been able to mediate differences, died. In June the Emperor began what is known as the One Hundred Days of Reform and set in motion a process that changed forever the history of the empire.

Marble boat built by Tz'u Hsi for her enjoyment with money designated for the navy.

Chapter 9

Ts'u Hsi
The Final Struggle (Part 3)

Tz'u-hsi, Empress Dowager
power behind the throne, 1861-1908

The Emperor's decrees followed one another in quick succession. His first act was shattering as it did away with the centuries old examination system that produced the mandarins of power, and at the same time he advised imperial clan members to go abroad and study politics. His edict created a sensation as century-old policies were challenged.

Other decrees followed. Practical subjects were to be included in examinations such as the history of other countries and contemporary politics. The morally corrupt Manchu troops were to be reorganized. High schools and colleges were to be founded in the provinces.

The appeal by the reactionaries to the Empress Dowager to stop these radical moves was met with a refusal, but Old Buddha kept a close watch through her appointees and the Conservatives set out to win her over.

The next step in the reform movement was a decree that ordered gazettes to be published all over the empire. They were official newspapers for the purpose of extending general knowledge, were to be government subsidized, and opinions were to be freely expressed and abuses exposed.

Next came an order for a naval college to reform and reconstruct the navy. Railway and mining bureaus were established and a Cantonese reformer was authorized to translate foreign works on political economy and natural sciences.

Then came a startling announcement that the Emperor and the Empress Dowager would travel BY TRAIN to Tientsin to review the troops. Conservatives were aghast, but the Old Buddha was intrigued by the novelty of a train ride.

Obsolete government offices were then abolished, which shattered the hundreds whose sinecures cost the state heavy financial burdens.

In shock, the Conservatives went en masse to the Summer Palace to beg Tz'u Hsi to resume supreme power. But the wise old Buddha said "Wait". The Emperor took this as indecision on her part. Meanwhile the reformers secretly pressed him to surround the Summer Palace, seize Tz'u Hsi and, after confining her, to strip her of all power. The Emperor agreed with the plot but suggested waiting until the train trip to Tienstsin.

But the reformers were unaware of a eunuch spy who reported the deliberations to the Dowager. It was necessary for her to get military support. Her old friend Jung Lu was back in power and in command of a strong body of troops. He was quietly summoned from Tientsin and plans laid for his detachment to support the Dowager.

Meanwhile more decrees followed ordering macademized roads to be built in Peking, the enrolment of militia for national defence, the granting of permission for Manchus to leave Peking to earn a living in the provinces, the teaching of European languages in public schools, and demands that more justice be dispensed in district courts. Finally, so that all might know that the Emperor cared for his people, all decrees were to be distributed nation-wide, and memorials to the Emperor were permitted outlining the needs of the people.

Whilst Tz'u Hsi was not opposed to some of the reforms, she feared for her power and the future of the dynasty. By August she had been won over by the reactionaries.

The Emperor was looking for an aggressive military leader who would participate in his plans. He settled on Yuan Shi-kai who was commissioned to kill Jung Lu, bring his own troops to Peking, and seize and imprison the Dowager. Yuan swore allegiance to the Emperor and agreed to the plot but on his way to Tientsin he reconsidered his situation. Unknown to the

Emperor, he and Jung Lu had become good friends and had sworn a bond of friendship as blood brothers. Moreover, the Emperor, in spite of his decrees, was considered too weak to control a stable government, and his actions against the Dowager would be a grave infraction of the rules of filial piety. Yuan shrewdly decided that in a contest between the Emperor and the Empress Dowager, the outcome was foreseeable. Yuan chose to betray the Emperor.

Arriving in Tientsin, Yuan went directly to Jung Lu who slipped quietly into Peking and went immediately to the Summer Palace to inform Tz'u Hsi. She sent secretly for the Conservatives who within two hours gathered in the Palace and were made aware of the situation. Guards at the Forbidden City were immediately replaced by Jung Lu's corps. Jung Lu returned to Tientsin to await orders.

The Empress issued a decree announcing that the Emperor was seriously ill and that she had been asked to resume power. The Emperor was placed under "house arrest" and was confined to a small island in the grounds of the palace. Several of his radical advisers were arrested and executed, and those who could, fled to Hong Kong or overseas for safety.

The fact that the Emperor enjoyed the support and sympathy of foreigners condemned him in the eyes of many Chinese and justified the Dowager's assumption of control. International opinion was strongly critical, the British indicating that action would be taken if the Emperor's life was endangered. But this was regarded by all Chinese as interference in a purely domestic affair.

Doctors were brought in, including a French physician, to attend T'ung Chih, which reassured the foreign community that the young Emperor was alive. However, the lack of an heir plunged the country again into instability.

Tz'u Hsi immediately took steps to rid the country of all those who had supported the reform program and whom she considered a threat to the Manchu dynasty. Jung Lu was then raised to the highest office in the military command.

Meanwhile the Emperor was presented at a lavish reception the Empress Dowager gave to the ladies of the Diplomatic Corps in Peking who declared the Dowager to be a most dignified and charming person. The Old Buddha had proved that the Emperor was alive and well and she had created, with her charm and elaborate gifts to the guests, a favourable impression of her kindness and goodwill. But the Emperor was returned to his confinement, a lonely and broken man. The Dowager then issued decrees purporting to show care and concern for her people, calling for justice and the conversion of criminals to a life of virtue, but at the same time reinstating many of the reactionaries who claimed to be the defenders of Confucian morality and traditional values.

Since the Emperor could not father an heir, Pu-chan, son of Prince Tuan, was adopted as the posthumous son of the previous Emperor, thus providing a successor who could make all the filial sacrifices so blatantly neglected when the Emperor had died. The youth, however, turned out to be unruly, uncouth and lecherous to the dismay of Old Buddha.

Meanwhile the Southerners were bitterly denouncing the Dowager and hinting that she was essentially anti-Chinese and that Manchus would eventually be appointed to all major posts in the realm. Her supporters therefore staged anti-foreign demonstrations believing this would please the Old Buddha. The encroachment of foreign powers on China's soil became increasingly repugnant to the government and to the people, who were humiliated by the treatment they received at the hands of the arrogant intruders. Their sense of injustice led to a cry for revenge and Tz'u Hsi was urged to take action. The work of missionaries was denounced, western medical treatment and operations were considered barbarous, foreign teachings were contrary to revered Chinese beliefs, and the protection of Christian teachers by foreign gunboats was deeply resented.

Secret societies, bound together by rituals, rites and oaths of allegiance to fight oppressors and exploiters, had always been very much a part of Chinese society. One such was the Righteous and Harmonious Fists who engaged in wrestling and the martial arts and eventually became known as the Boxers. One of their primary aims was to get rid of the foreign devils who had forced the government to surrender territory, had offended the spirits by building railways and engaging in mining, and had converted some of their countrymen to the offensive Christian beliefs that forbade idol and ancestor worship, reverence for Confucius, and participation in festivals that honoured local deities.

Added to these offences was the effect of the foreign invasion on the economic life of the country with the control of the Customs and the influx of goods that disrupted the local markets. Widespread famine, natural disasters and starvation added to the frustration and fuelled the desire for revenge. Reactionaries in the government were naturally very much in sympathy with the Boxer movement and certain officials gave their support. In January 1900, a decree was issued declaring that people practised in martial arts who were defending their villages were not bandits but legitimate protectors and were simply banded together for mutual aid. Consequently the Boxers became more militant, destroying railways and telegraphs as symbols of foreign penetration.

The first attack on foreigners was in December 1899, when a German missionary was murdered. The foreign Legations protested and for several months continued their demands for the suppression of the Boxers. The Western community did not believe that the massacre of foreign residents was imminent and although the diplomatic bodies in Peking received veiled warnings of danger, they were not sufficiently alarmed to take precautions. In May, 1900, a small detachment of 400 foreign soldiers and sailors was sent to Peking, but the Boxers were advancing in numbers and successfully cut off any further reinforcements by destroying the railway lines into Peking.

The first victims of the Boxer attack on Peking were the Chinese Christians, "The devil's disciples", who were burned to death in their homes. On June 20 a German diplomat left the Legation premises to intercede with the Boxers but was murdered, and by 4 p.m. that day the foreign Legations were under siege. The murder of missionaries throughout the country continued and the Legations in Peking were bombarded.

Although all China was united in the desire to expel the foreigners, the Southerners urged the government to negotiate with the foreign powers. Jung Lu urged restraint, refused to release the heavy guns under his control for the bombarding of foreign legations, and was consequently denounced as a traitor. The erratic official policy and the frenzied patriotic movement added momentum to the chaotic situation. Some brave men dared to offer wise counsel but were executed for their advice. Tz'u Hsi tried to play both sides, siding with the Boxers in their desire to push the foreigners out of China, yet realizing the necessity of insuring the continuation of her dynasty. Meanwhile allied troops landed in Tientsin and advanced on the capital.

At 4 o'clock in the afternoon of August 13 one of the Princes burst into the Forbidden City and cried,

"Old Buddha, the foreign devils have arrived."

Calmly Tz'u-Hsi began preparing to leave. By 3 a.m. she had changed her formal attire for peasant clothes, had summoned the Emperor and his Consort, the Imperial Princesses, Pu-Chun the heir apparent, and her favourite eunuch Li-lien-ying, urging them to do likewise, and had ordered carts to be ready to carry them to a safe haven.

The concubines were told that they would not go with the party, and when the Emperor's favourite begged that the Emperor be allowed to stay in Peking, Tz'u Hsi ordered her thrown down a well that it still pointed out today as the site of the murder.

The party joined the throng of people evacuating the ravaged city and journeyed unchallenged to the Summer Palace. After an overnight rest they set out again and reached the home of a district magistrate who, having lost most of his belongings to the rebels, was fearful of receiving Her Majesty. However, as no food had been available in the devastated areas along the way, the royal party was glad of simple fare, a bowl of millet porridge replacing the one hundred dishes ordinarily prepared for each meal for Tz'u Hsi. In spite of hardship and deprivation, the indomitable Old Buddha in her mid-sixties continued her journey at a leisurely pace, bound for the distant province of Shensi.

A message was sent ahead to the Governor to prepare a palace for her Majesty and meanwhile Old Buddha enjoyed the interest shown in her by the local populace, and stopped to view ancient temples and monuments along the way. In one centre she was entertained by a local Governor who presented a demonstration of how he had killed all the missionaries and their families in his district.

The Court finally reached Sianfu (Xian), the capital of Shensi, on October 28 and were joined by some officials, ministers and eunuchs who had managed to catch up with the party. Messengers were immediately dispatched ordering all Governors and Viceroys to send funds and tributes to Sianfu to maintain the Court and the troops.

When the allied troops entered Peking the Chinese resistance collapsed and the city was sacked by foreign soldiers. Priceless treasures were destroyed, and till this day the great golden urns in the Forbidden City show where gold was scraped off by the looters. National rivalries between the victors only added to the dismal scene. However, on September 7 the foreign powers finally forced China to accept the Protocol of 1901 that was a devastating document. Included was severe punishment of pro Boxer supporters, foreign control of trade, reparations for murders, demolition of strategic military bases, reform of protocol in foreign relations, and stupendous indemnities. Even some British commentators deplored the harsh terms that lacked any consideration for the crippling effects of the agreement on the people of China.

It was a year since the Empress Dowager had fled the capital but she was not prepared to return until she could do so on her own terms and in her own style. After much consultation with astrologers, the date was set for October 20. The imperial chariots left Sianfu escorted by a military bodyguard, the ranks of eunuchs who had deserted during the upheaval, the Court and ladies in attendance, followed by endless wagons carrying treasures and gifts of carpets, porcelains, carved furniture for refurbishing the palaces, and personal gifts of gold, silver, jade, jewels, furs and embroideries.

Pauses were made along the way to celebrate Old Buddha's sixty-sixth birthday and to enjoy theatrical performances of which she never tired. When the royal party crossed the Yellow River they did so in a gilt and lacquer barge in the shape of a dragon, especially built at great expense by the local authorities.

On the last lap of the journey Her Majesty was delighted with the arrangement to proceed by train, a trip she had longed to undertake for sometime. Awaiting the travellers were twenty-one train carriages, those for the royal party lavishly decorated and richly furnished with thrones, reception areas, and couches upholstered in imperial yellow silk.

When the train arrived in Peking at the newly constructed station, Emperor Pu Chun and the Empress Dowager were ushered into a lavish pavilion especially constructed and furnished with gold lacquer thrones and precious ornaments. The woman who had fled the city dressed as a peasant was returning in majestic style as head of state. The road from the station to Forbidden City was lined with kneeling troops, and many foreigners witnessed the procession from a vantage point. To their amazement Tz'u Hsi, whom they considered the epitome of evil, noticed them, smiled and made a gracious gesture of acknowledgement. The magnificence of the cortege, the pageantry, the seeming friendliness of Her Majesty impressed the foreign onlookers and seemed to foretell a new policy that might be a turning point in history.

Once the Court was re-established in the palace of the Forbidden City, work was begun rebuilding and restoring the vandalized quarters. Tz'u Hsi had wisely stored her personal fortune in wells and on her return they were found to be intact. The magnificent gifts brought from Sianfu helped to restore the palace to some of its former grandeur.

In April 1903, Jung Lu died and his death was a severe blow. In spite of her ruthless ambition Old Buddha had a deep affection for the man who had loved and served her so faithfully over the years. At the time of his death he had risen to the highest post in the realm, that of Grand Secretary and Grand Councillor, and posthumously he was awarded further honourable titles and a lavish funeral.

Overcoming her hatred of the foreign devils who had destroyed her city, the Empress Dowager set out to woo the diplomatic corps. Her receptions for the wives were more lavish than ever, and she noted with cynicism that her "honeyed sentiments" did much to wipe out the bitter memories of her support of the Boxers. The restored buildings and gardens with their appeal to elegance, the Empress with her charm and smile, captivated foreign visitors and led to a more friendly relationship and eventually forgiveness for much of the past.

The weight of government hung heavily upon the ageing Empress, made more poignant by Russian aggression and the consequent alignment of the other powers eager for slices of Chinese territory. Especially bitter was the feud between Russia and Japan over Manchuria, the ancestral home of the imperial family, the Manchus. War broke out and in 1904 Japan defeated Russia, a momentous event in East-West relations. Eventually the warring nations withdrew their troops but continued to use the railways for their own purposes.

Some of the edicts issued by the Emperor during the Hundred Days of Reform were recast and introduced, but the South was implacably opposed to Old Buddha's rule and began to work actively for the overthrow of her dynasty.

In August 1907 when she was 72, Tz'u Hsi suffered a mild stroke, but her speech and mental powers and her lust for despotic power suffered no decline. She began to talk of a constitution and of presiding over a parliament. Others considered that her days were numbered and that the Emperor, now in his late thirties, would take up the reins and resume his reform policies following the Japanese pattern of learning from the West. Some officials and eunuchs feared that should the Emperor come to the throne he might take revenge on those who had opposed or ill-treated him when he was helpless to retaliate. But strangely the Emperor took ill and died on November 14, 1908. Suspicion as always surrounded his death but no circumstantial evidence was ever found to prove the innuendoes. However, spies had reported to the Old Buddha that the Emperor had vowed on the death of the Dowager to execute the Chief Eunuch, Li Lien-ying, and that the Emperor had gloated over the Dowager's impending death.

Tz'u Hsi, determined to continue her rule, had chosen the little two-year old Pu-yi son of Prince Chun II, and grandson of Jung Lu, as the new emperor, and his father was appointed regent. Despite opposition, she had persuaded the Grand Council to accept her choice, explaining that she would be on hand to assist and guide Prince Chun. She then prepared edicts in the new Emperor's name, assigning titles to herself and the late Emperor's widow.

Plans were being made to celebrate the assumption of the new titles when Tz'u Hsi fainted at her luncheon meal. The pressures on her since the Emperor's death had been too much for her and she sensed her impending death. She issued a last decree, and, dressed in her ceremonial robes, died at 3 p.m. After 47 years of imperious rule the voice of dictatorship was stilled and the common people acknowledged the courage and tenacity of this last of the great Empresses.

Her funeral was a gorgeous spectacle and the treasures buried with her were worth a prince's ransom. Her body lay at rest until 1928 when the tomb was vandalized, the treasures stolen, and her body desecrated, an ignominious epilogue to a dramatic life story.

The Royal Family's summer palace.

Industrial Development of the Period

Building the first electric power house in Canton, 1904-1906

The introduction of electric streetcars, Shanghai 1907

The Soong Sisters Background

No account of famous women of China could omit the triumvirate of the Soong Sisters, Ai-ling, Ching-ling and Mei-ling. But to understand them one must look at a very brief account of their father, Charlie Soong, who, as a boy of 9, was sent to the U.S.A. in 1870 to apprentice in his uncle's store in Boston. His uncle, who had no sons, was a tea and silk merchant and adopted his nephew as his successor.

For three years Charlie obediently followed his uncle's plan but his friendship with some Chinese students raised his hopes of attaining an education. Uncle, however, was totally unsympathetic to such a ridiculous idea, insisting that Charlie follow the family plan for his life.

But Charlie hated his work, longed for an education, and finally stowed away on a southbound steamer. He was discovered by a kindly, pious captain who passed him on to the care of his Southern Methodist friends. A bright young oriental, complete with long queue was a unique phenomenon, and Charlie basked in the attention he received. The Methodist community began to instruct him in the Christian faith and saw an opportunity to convert a "heathen" and send him back to his homeland as a missionary.

Charlie was adopted into the home of General Carr, a rich textile manufacturer and philanthropist. Over the years the boy received an education, became a Christian, and eventually left the Carr home to enter Vanderbilt University in Nashville, Tennessee. He was a popular young man, exuding charm, and proved to be a clever and willing student.

Charlie returned to China in 1886 as a minister of the Southern Methodist Mission, teaching and preaching in areas around Shanghai. But Shanghai at that time was on the brink of a great period of industrial expansion, and Charlie's heart was tuned to this development. It was also the time when Dr. Sun Yat Sen was rising as the leader of the movement to modernize and revolutionize China. Charlie was totally sympathetic and not only donated to the revolutionary cause, but worked unceasingly on its behalf.

A year after his return, Charlie married the clever, well-educated daughter of an influential Christian family, and six children, three girls and three boys were born to the Soongs. The children were rigorously trained from earliest childhood, starting to learn Chinese characters at three or four years of age, and were drilled in the code of manners and trained in the Classics.

Meanwhile Charlie resigned from the Mission and entered the business world. He began to bring about changes in the industrial life of Shanghai, importing foreign machinery and attempting to improve the lot of workers. Eventually he set up a publishing house with Bibles as the chief output, but secretly turning out revolutionary tracts for Dr. Sun Yat Sen, a dangerous enterprise in that pre-revolutionary period.

Charlie's American ways were somewhat disconcerting to the people of Shanghai. His frankness, his unwillingness to practice the circuitous and often insincere conversational exchanges, and his distaste for elaborate Chinese conventions embarrassed his contemporaries but in the end they began to imitate his style. Moreover, his excellent connections in the United States made him sought after by both Chinese and foreigners and he became a very useful and successful go-between in the business world. His flour mill and noodle factory, his interests in tobacco and textile plants, his commercial press amassed him a personal fortune and much of his liquid assets he poured into the revolutionary coffers of Sun Yat Sen.

Mrs. Soong, a strong Christian, was notable for her "good works", her generosity to the poor and needy. As a mother she was a strict disciplinarian and ruled her home with an iron will. At the same time she recognized the need for her children to be sent away to school at an early age, the girls being treated in the same fashion as the boys.

Charlie Soong maintained his Christian fervour and attended services every Sunday with his wife. The children that were old enough were brought with their parents and enrolled in the Sunday School of which Charlie was superintendent.

At the same time, Charlie Soong was a member of one of the most powerful secret societies, always popular in Chinese society.

Chapter 10

Love of Money
Soong Ai Ling

Soong Ai Ling (seated second row left) 1912 at Christian Conference as secretary to Dr. Sun Yat Sen (seated beside her)

The first child born to Charlie and his wife was a daughter whom they named Ai-ling (Loving Mood). She is always described as a tomboy, and because of her vivaciousness often caused her mother considerable distress. But Ai-ling was her father's favourite and he took her everywhere with him. She was smart and quick to learn. She would sit in his office and watch as businessmen came to negotiate transactions and wheel and deal in investments. The lessons learned were not forgotten and in later years were very much a part of her adult mind set.

At five Ai-ling announced that she was ready for school. She was fascinated by the fact that the senior girls at the McTyiere School formed the church choir and always had a special place to sit. This appealed to her sense of position and power, dominant characteristics in her life. Her mother opposed the idea of her starting school at such an early age but Charlie introduced Ai-ling to Miss Richardson, Principal of McTyiere School For Girls, the most exclusive mission school in Shanghai. Miss Richardson already knew Ai-ling through the church and recognized her as a precocious youngster, old for her age. She accepted her as a special pupil to be personally tutored by Miss Richardson herself.

Ai-ling was to be a boarder and after a week of intense excitement, her trunk was packed and, in green trousers and plaid jacket, with her hair in pigtails and tied with ribbons, she left in a rickshaw for the school. Her grandmother protested at the cruelty of sending such a young child away from home, and her mother was none too happy, but Ai-ling and Charlie were determined and, her pockets filled with toffees and chocolates, she arrived at McTyeire.

When the moment for leave-taking arrived, Ai-ling clung to her father, sobbing, but Miss Richardson rocked the little girl in her lap and Ai-ling speedily recovered her calm. She became a popular mascot and was often called Madame Soong. During her second year at the school she was losing her baby teeth and the older girls teased her about her two front teeth being missing. But Ai-ling was equal to the situation and simply remarked that Madame Soong's two front gates had been stolen.

Life was not altogether easy. Being so small, Ai-ling found the big desks horribly uncomfortable and at the meal table she often could not reach the food that was set out in bowls, which meant she sometimes left the table hungry. In the evenings she was alone in bed while the older girls were studying, and she found the big dormitory frightening in its emptiness.

Summer holidays were spent at the family home and here she received training in other ways. But Ai-ling hated sewing and it was only her father's support that saved her from long hours of learning the art of embroidery. Charlie assured his wife that eyes were better employed in reading, and Ai-ling readily admitted in later life that she was hopeless at sewing.

Charlie Soong had a fine voice and Ai-ling and he often sang duets during the summer evenings, many of the songs that Charlie had picked up from his stay in America.

On her tenth birthday Ai-ling became one of the first Chinese girls to own a bicycle, and she would ride with her father up and down the streets of Shanghai, circling round the Sikh traffic policeman, to his great consternation.

This was the same year that the Boxer Rebellion broke out, and the Soongs were very concerned for their Christian friends. A further concern was for the life of a close friend, Kung Hsiang-hsi, who was to become Ai-ling's future husband. Unbeknown to his family he had become a Christian and a revolutionary, and when the Boxers were hunting down the foreigners, Kung set out to assist some of them to escape. Because of the illness of one of the foreign group, they were unable to leave and subsequently were all killed, but they had entrusted letters home to Kung's keeping. The Soong family was terrified lest he be discovered and they moved him from house to house for the duration of the rebellion. Finally he was able to leave for the States to deliver the letters personally, and there he remained for several years studying and imbibing western culture.

Once the Boxer Rebellion was crushed, Charlie began to consider his children's future. He was determined that they should all have an American education and when Ai-ling was thirteen she announced that she was ready to go to the States. Charlie felt that with a year's tutoring in America she would be ready to enter college. He approached one of his friends in the States and the up-shot was that Judge Guerry offered her accommodation in his home. Missionaries returning to the States on furlough agreed to take her with them, and so in May 1904, Ai-ling set sail for San Francisco. But when the wife of the missionary family took ill on the passage to Japan and the whole family disembarked to stay with the mother, Ai-ling was left to continue the journey alone under the eye of another missionary couple aboard.

On the ship Ai-ling experienced intense hatred towards Orientals and when she arrived in San Francisco her passport was inspected and declared irregular in spite of the fact that it was an authentic passport signed and sealed at the consulate in Shanghai. Immigration officials said she would be put in the detention shed, a disgusting building that housed violent cases; not fit for a fifteen year old girl.

The missionary in charge of Ai-ling refused to leave the girl, so the two were confined on board ship and promptly forgotten. After several days the missionary was able to go ashore and telephone friends who came to demand justice. But Ai-ling was moved from one ship to another for nineteen days, shedding occasional tears of anger and disillusionment but not succumbing to tearful self-pity. Finally through the efforts of a Presbyterian doctor she was freed and rejoined her earlier friends from

Shanghai who had arrived from the stopover in Japan. Tougher and wiser, and deeply wounded by her experience Ai-ling arrived in Macon ready to begin her studies at Wesleyan College as a "subfreshman".

The college catered largely to well-to-do southern families, and the girls dressed in elaborate style. Ai-ling was considered a serious student and her reserve was interpreted as shyness, but she was soon able to estimate the worth of the belongings of the other students and was not under any misapprehension as to their true value. But she also fascinated the girls with her clothes, and periodically Mrs. Soong would send chests of silk to her daughter and her classmates would gather round to "oo and ah" over the beautiful materials. Sometimes there were judicious trades for some of the homemade goodies that the American girls received.

Charlie kept her informed about her Chinese roots and she rebelled at any suggestion that she was a "fine American citizen." Her treatment by immigration had not endeared her to American citizenship.

In January 1906 Ai-ling was given permission to go to Washington to meet her uncle who had been sent on a special mission to the States. As girls in those days did not travel unattended, Judge Guerry's wife accompanied her. While in Washington Ai-ling went with her uncle to a White House reception where she was introduced to President Theodore Roosevelt who asked her what she thought of America.

"America is very beautiful," she replied, "and I am very happy here, but why do you call it a free country?" She then proceeded to describe the treatment she had received on her arrival. "Why should a Chinese girl be kept out of a country if it is so free. We would never treat visitors to China like that. America is supposed to be the Land of Liberty."

Needless to say, the President was somewhat taken aback and offered a brief apology.

From Washington she went with her uncle to New York where she met her father who had just arrived on a visit to his old friends in the States. In New York she also met Kung Hsiang-hsi who was then doing post-graduate work at Yale. Years later when they met in Japan he had not forgotten her.

Charlie was struck by Ai-ling's fashionable appearance and the maturity she had developed in the two years since she had left her homeland.

Back at college Ai-ling once again joined in activities, including drama classes, and she gave a reading at her graduation exercises. She graduated in

1909 at the age of 19 with an enviable record of high marks. She then returned to Shanghai, leaving behind her younger sisters, 15 year old Ching-ling and 8 year old Mei-ling who had joined her in the States the previous year. Charlie was aware that his revolutionary conspiracies might lead to his arrest and even execution and he was anxious that his children be out of danger. His oldest son was finishing high school in Shanghai and would soon be entering Harvard University. The two younger boys could easily be moved out of harm's way if necessary but the girls were sent to America for safety sake, and also because an American education was part of Charlie's plans for his girls.

On her return to China Ai-ling found her father had set up a desk for her in his study and another in his print shop. She was assigned to be Dr. Sun Yat Sen's secretary, handling all his correspondence and coded messages, and polishing his speeches and public announcements. At first Ai-ling met with criticism and resentment. Young girls did not behave in such a forward way. Her style, her education, her command of English set her apart. But Ai-ling was tough, and eventually she was accepted and paved the way for her brothers and sisters.

In October 1911 fateful days arrived. The accidental explosion of a homemade bomb sent the police to the headquarters of the garrison that was plotting an uprising. There was no choice. The rebels did what Dr. Sun had been trying to do for years: they started a revolution. One province after another joined the rebels and the imperial dynasty was overthrown. China was in a state of chaos. But Dr. Sun emerged as the leader and on January 1, 1912, he became the first President of the Provisional Government of the Republic of China.

However, it soon became evident that Sun was not strong enough for the job and he resigned in favour of strong man Yuan Shi-kai. But Yuan, in control of the army, took over power and the Sun revolution was in jeopardy. Sun fled to Japan, as did the whole Soong family, along with another of Sun's supporters, Chiang Kai-shek. It seemed that the revolution had fallen apart, but its supporters were determined to rebuild.

In Tokyo the Soongs met Kung Hsiang-hsi who had just returned from the States and was working with the YMCA. He recalled meeting Ai-ling in New York. Ai-ling found him to be a realist and one to whom money was important. She regarded money as the purchase price of power. She had seen what money had done for her American friends and for her father and she craved the power that it brought. The two young people had found like-minded mates. Their friendship blossomed and they were married at a quiet ceremony in a little church in Yokohama. Dr. Kung's ambition was to found a school to train people to carry out the principles of democracy. When Yuan died suddenly in 1915, Sun and his followers were free to return to China although the country was plunged into civil war.

Kung set out for his home province of Shansi to prepare a home for his bride and to set up the school that he had been planning for a long time. Ai-ling stayed with her parents in Shanghai until Kung came to fetch her and she began her first trip into the interior of China. Roads were non-existent in many areas and once they reached the end of the railway line Ai-ling had to be carried in a sedan chair. She dreaded what awaited her, fearing the primitive conditions, but to her surprise she found the Kung family house in Taiku was like a palace, and it was in that city that important bankers lived and conducted business.

Dr. Kung immediately began to set up his school with the modernization of his province of Shansi in mind. When the school was built and everything was ready, Kung found himself short of teachers. Someone dared to suggest that Ai-ling was qualified, but the thought of a young woman taking over the responsibilities of a revered schoolmaster and teaching men was met with consternation. The school, however, was admittedly different and since Ai-ling was a member of the Kung family she was finally accepted and taught English and health.

It was while living in Taiku that Ai-ling gave birth to their first child, Rosamonde. Shortly afterwards the family moved and three more children, David, Jeanette and Louis were born in Shanghai.

Dr. Kung's financial ability led him to new fields and he became Commissioner of Finance for the province of Kwantung and Minister of Industry for the government. With the rise of communism in the early 20's and the growing power of Chiang Kai-shek, the Shanghai bankers, including Kung and Ai-ling, threw their support behind Chiang. Ai-ling became the mastermind behind an alliance of family and wealth and eventually arranged for her youngest sister, Mei-ling to marry Chiang Kai-shek.

Meanwhile Kung was amassing a fortune as principal agent for Standard Oil Company in China, serving on boards of directors of various companies, and acting as go-between for the various warlords. Ai-ling became the administrator of the Kung fortune, using her husband's positions to gain financial information that translated into personal wealth. She was regarded by many foreigners as a strong-willed, cunning and ambitious woman who became one of the most powerful forces in the country. She and her husband were known to squeeze money from terrified merchants, at the same time winning the admiration and support of American friends. During World War II the Soong family was reputed to have made a fortune out of the lend-lease aid to China, and FBI documents, investigating the allegations, report that "Madame Kung is an evil and clever woman who is reputed to have hired assassins in China and has cleverly hood-winked the Americans." Chinese commentators are known to have called her "The most hated woman in China."

In June 1944 Ai-ling accompanied her sister Mei-ling on a trip to Brazil where she had dealings with the Brazilian dictator and acquired rich properties in industrial areas. The trip was undoubtedly intended to spread the Soong fortune around South America in oil, shipping and transportation. At the same time, Dr. Kung, who was then Minister of Finance for China, was fired from his post on the pretext of his being sent on a special assignment to the States. Obviously a power struggle had been going on and the Kungs lost, but considering the Soongs were reputed to have amassed the largest fortune in the world, life abroad was no great hardship. It was estimated that Kung and Ai-ling together were worth at least $1 billion U.S., most of which had been expeditiously moved out of China. But for China, Kung's "funny money" policies and Ai-ling's profiteering had created astronomical inflation. Constantly fluctuating currencies made it difficult to assess the value of foreign aid.

In 1947 the Kungs visited their estates in Taiku, liquidated their holdings and Dr. Kung announced that he was moving to New York where Ai-ling. who was "not feeling well", would be close to medical attention. When Chiang Kai-shek was forced out of China by the Communists in 1949 and took over Taiwan, the Kungs were the pipeline for American connections with the Taiwanese government.

In 1966 Dr. Kung, at the age of 84, developed a severe heart condition and died on August 15. Ai-ling survived six more years, dying at the age of 85 in New York, but only a short obituary in the New York Times commented on this woman who so cunningly amassed an enormous fortune, arranged marriages of political significance, and was the principal architect of the Soong dynasty.

Education for girls who could afford it, 1905

Chapter 11

Love of Country
Soong Ching-Ling

Soong Ching Ling (left)

Ching-ling (happy mood), the second of the Soong sisters, was born in Shanghai on January 27, 1893. She was a totally different person to her elder sister: a quiet girl interested in learning and ideas. In physical make-up she was not plump like her sisters but had the delicate beauty admired by the Chinese. Unlike Ai-ling with her imperious airs, she was gentler and more gracious. In 1900 when she had just turned seven, she followed Ai-ling to McTyeire and proved to be an industrious student. The high standards of McTyeire made the Soong sisters very proficient in English and the opportunity to speak English at home with their father increased their proficiency.

In 1908 Ching-ling and her younger sister, Mei-ling, who was then only nine years of age, were sent under the care of their uncle and aunt to Macon in the U.S., where Ailing was studying. Mei-ling was too young to be a regular student and stayed with the President's family on campus while Ching-ling at fifteen became an undergraduate, specializing in philosophy. She was a hard worker but her time spent in study did not prevent her from making lasting friends. She kept in touch with her father and with events at home. An essay she produced, which was published in The Wesleyan, a student literary magazine, in November 1911, was entitled "The Influence of Foreign Education Students on China" in which she pointed out the effect that foreign training had on promotion of reform in China.

The year this essay was published was the year of revolution in China. Ching-ling's revered hero, Dr. Sun Yat Sen and the Soong family began to pick up the shattered pieces and try to set up a government to take over the floundering country. In America Ching-ling, inspired by the revolution, again published an article in the school paper entitled "The Greatest Event of the Twentieth Century."

In the spring of 1913, after her graduation, she returned home with gifts and letters for Dr. Sun from American friends. Her meeting with Sun, a national hero and her father's best friend, increased her admiration for the revolutionary leader.

But the rise to power of the military leader, Yuan Shi Kai, destroyed the gains of the revolution, and Sun and the Soongs fled to Japan and began slowly to rekindle the flame of reform. As Ai-ling was now married and had resigned as Dr. Sun's secretary, Dr. Sun invited Ching-ling to take her place. In daily contact with her hero, Ching-ling threw herself wholeheartedly into the "second revolution", the attempt by Sun and his supporters to revitalize the reform movement and win back the country. The passion with which they pursued their plans carried over into their personal relationships. Sun, a married man and nearly fifty years of age, and Ching-ling just twenty, were secretly planning marriage.

At this point the Soongs left Japan to return to their home in Shanghai. Ching-ling opposed the move but Charlie insisted, and the family took refuge in the French concession. Charlie then announced the formal engagement of his daughter Ching-ling to a young man of a good family, but she resisted and refused to go through with the marriage. Charlie confined her to the house but she wrote secretly to Sun who was still in Japan, asking if she could join him there. Sun wrote back saying that he needed her but that neither Charlie nor his own wife would condone such a marriage. As Christians they could not accept such an arrangement. Although Chinese marriage ties were not always considered binding, the Soongs did not approve of this loose interpretation, nor did they approve of Sun, who was also a Christian, abandoning his wife of many years for a young girl. To become a second wife in Chinese society could only come about when the family head arranged and approved the decision. Moreover, to Christians, a second wife was abhorrent.

But Ching-ling was not to be dissuaded so Charlie locked her in her bedroom. However, with the help of her loyal servant, she climbed out of the window and sailed at once for Japan. Ching-ling's will power and her determination to hold to her own decisions was a precursor of her later resolution and independence of thought.

When she arrived in Japan, Sun assured her that he had gone through divorce proceedings, which relieved her mind as she had been concerned about the scandal that might harm the revolutionary cause if she became his concubine. The Soongs did not believe that Sun had actually divorced his wife, and they considered that he was committing bigamy and that Ching-ling was an adulteress. Charlie followed Ching-ling to Japan but the marriage had already been performed. He challenged Sun and Ching-ling in a bitter confrontation, reminding Sun of their friendship and the years they had spent in struggle together, but to no avail. He then disowned Ching-ling and swore to have no more to do with Sun Yat Sen.

When Sun and Ching-ling eventually returned to Shanghai, the family avoided them, although they did set aside their bitterness when an old friend from the States came to visit. But shortly after this, in May 1918, Charlie at the age of 52 died suddenly of what was designated as stomach cancer, although he had not appeared ill for any length of time. Whether Charlie was poisoned by his enemies or it was a natural death due to strain and grieving that broke his spirit, has never been determined.

Meanwhile the revolutionary forces were breaking up into right and left wings. The treatment of China at the Versailles treaty conference after World War II gave birth to the May Fourth Movement which was supported by liberals and many professionals. The revolution was taking a new path and many were disturbed. In 1919 a group of radicals, in sympathy with and supported by the Russians, decided to form a Chinese Communist Party.

During this period Sun was concentrating his attention on the southern province of Kwangtung where he was highly respected, and in 1920 Ching-ling joined her husband in Canton. Sun's supporters elected him President of China, in name if not in fact, and Sun set out to enlarge his sphere of influence. He organized a northern expedition, and with the intrepid Ching-ling accompanying him in 1922 he proceeded north. As soon as he left, disloyal troops occupied Canton and Sung and Ching-ling hurried back to the city. But they walked into the jaws of danger, and Ching-ling in an article in a Chinese magazine later described the harrowing experience of escaping during the night, crawling along a bridge in the dark, avoiding fire from the enemy who were screaming, "Kill Sun, Kill Sun." When she saw blood-thirsty soldiers approaching her she lay on the ground pretending to be dead. Somehow she and her husband managed to make their way to a house on the riverfront and, disguised as peasants, boarded a ship for Hong Kong.

Before long they were back in Shanghai at a time when the Russians were courting the Chinese, calling on the Chinese masses to seek independence and rid themselves of foreign domination. A diplomatic mission under Joffe was sent to China, but receiving little encouragement in Peking, Joffe proceeded to Shanghai where, in January of 1923, Ching-ling and Sun entertained him. The Russians persuaded the Suns that Russia had no designs on China, and that the Nationalist Party which Sun headed was engaged in a struggle that Moscow could endorse.

Sun and Ching-ling supported by northern troops, set out again for Canton. The disloyal forces retreated and the couple was again in residence in the city. True to their commitment, the Russians sent an envoy to discuss the reorganization of Dr. Sun's Nationalist party, and to offer finances and help in training a powerful army. The Communist party in China was not asked to unite with the Nationalists but they were urged to get behind the Nationalists to bring about a truly national revolution.

Sun's control of Canton was not strong, but he found in Chiang Kai-shek a committed soldier whom he sent to Moscow in August 1923 to receive military training. But Chiang was disillusioned and in November returned to China. The following month he was appointed head of the military academy in Canton. Classes began in May 1924 with an official celebration attended by Ching-ling and Dr. Sun. With financial support from Russia, the academy was on its way to becoming the most powerful force in China, but in the end Sun was forced out of Canton and the Nationalist Army took over control.

Meantime an Army General sympathetic to Sun offered to set up Sun as the President of China if he would come to Peking. In December 1924, accompanied by Ching-ling, Sun arrived in Tientsin, port city of Peking. But on arrival Sun collapsed in great pain. For three weeks Ching-ling stayed by his bedside, and then on December 31 a special train took him to Peking where a massive crowd of thousands of well wishers greeted him. But he was too ill to speak to them and within a week he was diagnosed by specialists as having inoperable cancer of the liver.

Of all the millions of dollars he had raised for his beloved country, his personal will conveyed to Ching-ling all that he had left, his books and papers, a few personal items and the house he owned in Shanghai. On March 12, 1925, he died and his body lay in state for two weeks while half a million people came to honour their revolutionary leader. The funeral service was characterised by references to the revolutionary teachings of Christ who came to save the poor and broken-hearted and to bring freedom and universal brotherhood. Sun was buried on the Purple Mountain outside the city of Nanjing, and his tomb and statue continue to this day to draw a stream of visitors to honour the man called "The Father of Modern China."

Ching-ling now saw herself as the guardian of Sun's dream. Like her husband she had never committed herself to the Communist cause, but she felt she must support in the best way she could the principles for which her husband had stood. Anna Louise Strong, writing of Ching-ling said, "though in manner courteous almost of softness, she has in her a vein of iron."

In 1927 Chiang Kai-shek began his march north in an attempt to unify the country, but he betrayed the cause with a devastating attack on the communist and labour union supporters in Shanghai. Ching-ling spoke out against the atrocities and without doubt her life was in great danger. However, she remained calm and spoke of her sorrow for those who had strayed from the true path of reform. As she spoke for the great masses of people her popularity was enormous, but she seemed to be the lone voice opposing the regime of Chiang Kai-shek, and she was estranged from her own family. The man with whom she was working was seized by Chiang and tortured to death and she publicly denounced the political murder. More murders were committed when Chiang arrested members of the League of Left Writers, had them dig a pit, then tied their hands and feet and buried them alive.

When in 1932 the Japanese invaded Manchuria, Chiang Kai-shek made no effort to curb their advance. His chief concern was to hound the Communists and rid the country of "these bandits." Civil strife continued until the Japanese made their move into China in 1937, but even at this point Chiang still considered the Communists his chief enemies. Meanwhile

Mao Tse-tung had mobilized the communist forces and had led his supporters on the Lord March to north China where he set up a government. Ching-ling, like many others, was forced by the Japanese bombing to flee to the interior city of Chungking. Here she met with American advisers and warned them of the misuse of Lend-lease, largely by her own family members, but little attention was given to her accusations.

When the war with Japan ended, the Communist forces began their campaign of conquest, and by this time there was only one member of the Soong family left in China, Ching-ling. On October 1, 1949, when the great celebration of Liberation was held in Peking, Mao-Tse-tung stood in front of the Forbidden City to proclaim the People's Republic of China, with Ching-ling at his side. At 57 years of age she had survived the years of purges, torture and loneliness, had scorned a life of ease overseas as she could well have enjoyed, and now she was to dedicate herself to the people of China particularly the women and children.

Madame Soong Ching-ling became one of the three non-communist leaders chosen as Vice-Chairmen of the Central Government of Peking, but her great joy was working with and for the children of her homeland. The China Welfare Institute that she had founded in the earlier days became one of her dearest projects. During the war the international Peace Hospital had been one of her concerns and later she was instrumental in the establishment of maternity and child health hospitals. "All my life has been connected with children," she said "because children represent the future of China." From these enterprises grew programs in maternal and child hygiene, family planning services, classes for parents, child care, child education, Children's Palaces, Art Theatres and a children's magazine. Later she encouraged the publication of an adult magazine, *China Reconstructs*, now known as *CHINA TODAY* which is published in many languages and is read world-wide.

Another of her concentrated efforts was in the interests of international peace and understanding. For her work in establishing friendly relations with other countries, the President and members of the Board of Governors of the University of Victoria, in Victoria, British Columbia, Canada, journeyed to China in 1980 to confer on Soong Ching-ling the honorary degree of LLD. They also established a scholarship in her name at the university, which each year is given to a Chinese student recommended by the Chinese Association for Friendship with Foreign Countries.

As I was intending to visit China in May 1981 I wrote to Madame Soong, not realizing how ill she was, and asked if a few of us might visit her. I received a most gracious reply saying that she was not able to receive visitors but wishing us a pleasant visit to her homeland. After we arrived in China we learned with great sorrow on May 29 that she had just died of leukemia. On television we watched as the nation mourned the passing of a woman who through all the vicissitudes of China's agony, had remained dedicated to her people and their destiny. The whole nation paid tribute to its beloved, enduring patriot. Her home in its park-like setting, and naturally with a children's playground, is today a mecca for all those who respect her contribution to her motherland.

Following her death foreign friends established the Soon Ching Ling Children's Foundation, which is internationally supported, with branches in many countries around the world. Canada has a Foundation which is active in many cities and supports the humanitarian and educational goals so dear to Soon Ching Ling's heart.

Helping children with reading lessons at a literacy class

THE HISTORY AND MISSION OF
The Soong Ching Ling Children's Foundation of Canada

Soong Ching Ling, or Mme. Sun Yat-sen (1893-1981) is internationally acclaimed as one of the 20th century's most renowned woman leaders. She was loved and revered for her dedication to the emancipation of the Chinese people from domestic and foreign oppression, and to international peace and good will. One of her greatest concerns was the protection of children, their education and welfare, for which she worked tirelessly all her life.

After her death on May 29, 1981, members of her family, friends and admirers in different parts of the world set up independent Soong Ching Ling foundations to honour her memory and carry on her work for the children. There are already such foundations in Beijing, Shanghai, Canada, Japan and Hungary.

The Soong Ching Ling Children's Foundation of Canada was founded in 1981, a few months after her passing, as a voluntary, non-political, non-profit Foundation. It is devoted to linking the people of Canada and China for the education, health and welfare of children in both countries, in the spirit of international cooperation which Soong Ching Ling's life personified.

The Foundation puts priority on programmes in China which meet needs, reach out to help the underpriviledged and poor and enable local agencies to train their own personnel for solving their own problems. Similar programmes may be undertaken in Canada where the Foundation can play a unique role in enhancing cross cultural understanding. Special programmes should be developed to make the people of Canada aware of the needs of children in China.

The Soong Ching Ling Children's Foundation of Canada is dedicated to the cause of humanitarianism through education and improvement of the lives of children in China and Canada.

Chapter 12

Love of Power
Soong Mei-ling

Soong Mei-ling

Mei-ling (beautiful mood), born in 1897, was the youngest of the three Soong sisters. She was a plump infant who waddled around, impervious to bumps and falls because of her padded clothes and layers of fat. Her uncles called her "little lantern." She tended to vanity, was high strung and bossy, and liked to rule the household.

As soon as she turned five Mei-ling insisted that she join her sisters at McTyeire school and so she was sent off with her trunk to be a boarder and attend kindergarten. But her stay was short. During the day she seemed happy enough and was popular with staff and students, but at night alone in the dormitory, she had fits of trembling and was terrified by nightmares. She had to be sent home and was privately tutored until she went at the age of nine to the States in company with her 15-year old sister, Ching-ling.

As Mei-ling was too young to attend college, she stayed with the College President's family on campus. The President had a young daughter the same age and together with a third child living nearby the threesome formed a happy group. Not that there were no skirmishes, for Mei-ling was quick tempered, and when asked if she wasn't ashamed of her behaviour she assured her inquisitor that she really quite enjoyed it. Somehow her quick wit seemed to bewitch her elders and she relied on her popularity more than hard work to see her through. However, the special tutoring that she received enabled her to make faster progress than might have been possible in an ordinary classroom. She was undoubtedly very quick to learn and adapted to life in America more easily than her two sisters.

Mei-ling did not take the interest in affairs in China that Ching-ling did, being more concerned with classes and social activities. The Revolution of 1911 that inspired her older sister did not touch Mei-ling. She was still too young to appreciate its significance. When these stirring events were occurring in China, Mei-ling was completing her schooling and in 1913, after Ching-ling had graduated and returned to China, Mei-ling transferred to Wellesley College in Massachusetts where she was close to her older brother studying at Harvard. During her four years at college she grew from a plump teen-ager to a slim, attractive woman, specializing in English literature, philosophy and elocution.

Mei-ling was popular with the boys, many of them Chinese students from nearby colleges. When she heard of Ching-ling's elopement she was terrified that her parents might attempt to forestall any move of their youngest daughter to behave in such a disgraceful way and would arrange a marriage for her on her return to China. So anxious was she to avert such a situation that she became engaged to Peter Li, but once her anxiety had been overcome she broke off the engagement.

In 1917 Mei-ling graduated and returned to Shanghai where she became very popular and well known. Following her father's death in 1918 she carried on his crusading spirit in the form of public service. Having grown accustomed to the western life style she was shocked by the squalor and suffering she found in her homeland. It inspired her to work for social reform and she became a member of various community committees, including the Board of the YWCA and the Child Labour Commission. She was not so interested in the political aspects of Chinese life but was eager and impatient to carry out the reforms that were crying out for attention.

It was at this time that Chiang Kai-shek was moving to the fore in Chinese politics. Having been trained in the National Army School and with a three year period of training in Japan, he was commissioned to serve in the revolutionary forces when the 1911 revolution proved successful.

However, his violent temper, dissipation, and membership in brutal gangs that controlled brothels, arms, and appointments, made him anathema to the more idealistic revolutionaries. But with some military successes and the support of the gangs, he gained power and rose to be a senior lieutenant.

Chiang's love life was anything but admirable. His village wife was cast aside, his chambermaid concubine was discarded, and he fell madly in love with a captivating harlot whom he actually married in November of 1921. But the following month he attended a Christmas party given by one of the Soong sons and met Mei-ling. Her excellent connections and attractive personality led him to formulate plans for a courtship. He decided to ask Dr. Sun to promote an alliance, assuring him that he had divorced his wife and thrown out his concubine, but omitting to tell him of his recent marriage. He insisted that he had reformed his life and was now thoroughly dedicated to the revolution.

"Do you think Miss Soong would accept me?" he asked.

Dr. Sun did not think there was the slightest possibility but he said that he would consult his wife, Ching-ling. But Ching-ling was furious.

"I would rather see my little sister dead than married to a man with his reputation" was her reply.

Sun's polite reply to Chiang was "Wait a while", and this the would-be suitor did, for almost ten years.

During these years Chiang visited Russia and in 1924 became Commandant of the Whampao Military Academy set up by the Nationalist Party. With the help of foreign experts, particularly from the USSR, China began to develop a modern mechanized army

On the death of Sun Yat Sen there began a mad scramble for power. The leading right wing mastermind, fearing reprisals, fled with his supporters. This situation opened up the way for Chiang Kai-shek, with the help of underworld gangs, to take over and make himself dictator of China. At the same time, through a middleman, he actually proposed marriage to Ching-ling, Dr. Sun's widow. Needless to say, she refused.

In 1926 Chiang began his northern expedition and successfully established his power as he moved northward. The following year his treachery in Shanghai when he massacred the union and community groups that had massed to greet him, was the beginning of an all out war between the Communists and Nationalists. Labour leaders, students, left-wing newspapers were all decimated. The merchants and bankers guilds lent Chiang millions of dollars to protect them from "the reds", and Chiang set up his government in Nanking. America applauded Chiang's moves and many foreigners rejoiced at the defeat of the leftists.

Terrorist tactics kept money flowing into Chiang's coffers. The Soong family were divided in their allegiance, with Ai-ling and her husband H. H. Kung as Chiang's supporters while brother T. V. Soong opposed him, and sister Ching-ling was hundreds of miles away out of his reach. Meanwhile Chiang was assiduously courting Mei-ling and she finally accepted but would not marry without her mother's consent. But her mother strongly opposed the marriage. Chiang was a soldier, a class low in the Chinese scale, his relationships with other women was highly abhorrent, and most important, he was not a Christian. However, Ai-ling masterminded the alliance, and Chiang's proof of divorce and his willingness to study the Bible, finally wore down Mrs. Soong's opposition and the engagement was announced. The very ostentatious wedding took place on December 1, 1927 and Mei-ling became the First Lady of China. She and Chiang did their best to portray themselves as the heirs of Dr. Sun Yat Sen. The marriage was obviously one of convenience, but Mei-ling felt she could help Chiang to unify China and her position would get her a chance to introduce the reforms she desired.

Mei-ling accompanied her husband to Nanking, the new capital, where there was little social life as most of the government wives preferred to remain in Shanghai. But Chiang insisted that Mei-ling accompany him to official functions although she was often the only woman present. The city of Nanking had little to offer but Mei-ling was determined to bring some constructive results out of China's chaos. Education for children of the revolutionaries who had died in battle, rural service clubs, a club for officers to relieve the boredom of military life were all activities that she fostered, at the same time encouraging her husband in the study of Christian teachings.

But the consolidation of power was not complete and Chiang set off on another campaign, accompanied by Mei-ling. For the first time she saw conditions in the interior and it only strengthened her desire to "clean up the dirt" that constantly troubled her.

Chiang's success was troubling the Japanese. They had no desire to see a strong united China. When Chiang entered Peking and China was united in 1928, Chiang's name was known in every major capital in the world.

But new problems surfaced. The generals who had served under Chiang all wanted a share of the spoils, and leaders in outlying areas were not anxious to see central control.

Mei-ling was with her husband at all times, acting as his secretary, interpreting when necessary, discussing the problems that beset him, and teaching him English and the Bible. Finally Chiang agreed to become a Christian and was baptized in the home of Mrs. Soong. Everyone in the family was present with the exception of Ching-ling.

With the Japanese incursion into Manchuria, Chiang was faced with another threat. But he was reluctant to take action against a Japanese army when the persistent communist pressure was his primary concern. A strong protest was voiced at his non-resistance, and rumours were circulated that he had made a secret deal with the invaders.

It was at this point of time that the New Life Movement was born, its main tenets being modesty and economy of dress, cleanliness, moderation, and an attempt to revive the old moral values. Postage stamps were issued with the characters for Justice, Honesty, Propriety and Trust in the four corners. Railway cars outfitted with projectors were attached to trains and were dropped off for a day or two in each town where uplifting and informative movies were shown on roadside screens. Mei-ling was in her element, organizing, planning, receiving reports, and working with an American adviser. Chiang called for a million new school teachers, and high school graduates rushed to training colleges. The high school graduate club that I had founded for the girls of the school where I taught in Canton, disintegrated as the majority of members registered at night school to prepare for the great educational boom that was expected.

In October 1934, Chiang and Mei-ling decided to make a tour of some of the major cities, an unprecedented event. Laying stress on their New Life Movement, they made a point of inviting missionaries for coffee and conversation, made more intimate by Mei-ling's command of English. The visitors were favourably impressed, as they had never before been able to talk with even minor officials, let alone the acknowledged head of state.

The tour held many benefits. Chiang became acquainted with the hinterland and with the problems faced there, and the general populace had an opportunity to actually see the man who was their ruler. The trip did more to cement the solidarity of the country than all the military conquests. For Mei-ling it was an opportunity for her to emerge as a co-leader with her husband. As she made speeches to the women, urging them to take part in the national reform movement, she became even more committed to developing a sense of community responsibility for ridding the country of squalor and degrading habits.

The Chiang popularity was at its height. My husband was teaching in Hong Kong and the students were sporting Chiang buttons. He had to come to an agreement with his classes that if Chiang's name was mentioned they would not stand en masse and salute.

The following year the Japanese incursions into north China became even more menacing, and many felt that the invaders would move further south after consolidating their gains in the north. But Chiang was obsessed with the threat of the communists and preferred to spend his time and strength in their pursuit.

In 1935 Mao began his famous Long March to the northwest with Chiang's forces in pursuit, and Japan continued her insidious control of China's northern provinces. Intellectuals and students became angry, some newspapers dared to criticize, and some of Chiang's supporters were assassinated.

In October 1936 Chiang went to Xian to confer with one of his Marshals and then met Mei-ling in Loyang for a celebration of his fiftieth birthday. Returning to Xian in December for further consultations, an extraordinary incident occurred that shook the nation. Chiang was kidnapped by the Marshall and another General, and was told that the time had come to stop the anti-red campaign and to unite with the communist forces for a patriotic war against the common enemy, Japan. Chiang was held hostage and eight demands were made which included government reorganization, the end of civil war, free expression, the carrying out of Dr. Sun's principles, and the setting up of a National Salvation Conference.

Mei-ling fainted when she heard the news, but quickly revived and, against the advice of friends and officials, set out for Xian. Mao Tse-tung sent Chou En-lai to represent the Communist Party and Mei-ling was impressed by his grasp of issues. Finally Chiang grudgingly agreed to the terms, and it is generally agreed that the Soong family wealth helped to ease the decision for Chiang's release. He and Mei-ling and the official party that had gathered in the city, flew off to Nanking at 3 p.m. on December 25.

My husband and I and our six months old son were at a Christmas dinner party when Hong Kong erupted in a hail of firecrackers. Everyone had been concerned during the tense days of negotiations, and there was public rejoicing following the release of the still popular Chiang and admiration for Mei-ling's bravery in joining her husband.

Mei-ling was concerned about the loyalty of the Chinese air force, and she informed her husband that she would like to take over control. Chiang agreed and she was put in charge. She hired American advisers, among them the controversial Chennault, who was horrified at the corruption in the force and the dismal condition of the planes.

Mei-ling now began to play on the American conscience. The West was letting China down, she asserted, while her husband as a true Christian soldier was trying to stem the onslaught of both Reds and Japanese.

In the summer of 1937 the Japanese provoked a confrontation and the Sino Japanese conflict became a reality. My husband and I and our son were in Korea on holiday and by the time we left Korea, crossed Japan and took ship for Hong Kong via Shanghai, the Japanese had reached and occupied Shanghai and bombs were falling all around us. Once we reached Hong Kong we were out of the immediate conflict, but every night we heard bombers blasting Canton and the bridges connecting that city to Hong Kong. Hong Kong was on the alert and making provisions for an eventual Japanese attack.

Meanwhile the frightened Chinese government had fled to Chungking, leaving the capital Nanking to be raped by the invaders. Mei-ling and her sister, Ai-ling with her husband H. H. Kung, and T. V. Soong the eldest brother, now began to play on their American contacts and were soon able to get millions of dollars in lend-lease and other benefits to bolster their regime. American flyers suspected blatant fraud and corruption and the stockpiling of resources to renew war against the Communists. In fact thousands of soldiers were tied up in trying to prevent the Communists from attacking the Japanese.

After the attack on Pearl Harbour and the entry of the U.S. into the war in 1942, American aid was less forthcoming. It was left to Mei-ling to woo the American public and to be the chief informant to the world about the war in China. Wendell Wilkie had set the stage by his favourable reporting on his visit to China, and Mei-ling was being compared to famous military heroines of the past. She broadcast indignant speeches blaming the West for failure to help China and for allowing treaties to be breached that led to the murder of her countrymen. She questioned the sincerity of civilized nations claiming to be Christian, and asked if they were overawed by Japanese power, Her sentimental references to the tragedies of war made good copy in western magazines designed to move the indolent West.

Under the strain of wartime conditions Mei-ling's health began to deteriorate and it was decided that she should seek medical advice in the United States. A Boeing 307 was commandeered and, accompanied by two American nurses and her 18-year old niece, Mei-ling set off. She spent nearly three months in hospital but on her release she was invited to the Roosevelt's home where she prepared for an address to the American Congress. But her stay was not altogether a happy one. Her imperious manner and personal demands created problems for both the staff and her hosts, but her appearance before the Congress, beautifully dressed and groomed, was a sensational success, and the speech, both in content and presentation, aroused the American public.

Henry Luce controlled much of the press and he arranged a speaking itinerary for Mei-ling in many of the major cities. Through his publications he raised large sums of money and helped to consolidate the various China Relief Agencies into a single body so that more than seventeen million dollars poured in from all over the States. Nobody in America seemed to realize the economy of China was in such a state of inflation that the donated money was worth little except for some Chinese officials who made huge profits on the black market.

Mei-ling returned to Chungking in the summer of 1943 to join her husband on his trip to the Cairo Summit, but the Chiangs were not highly regarded. The British did not consider Chiang an effective statesman, and Churchill did much to persuade Roosevelt to disregard Chiang as an effective ally. Mei-ling had so antagonized the Roosevelts when she was in the States that the American President found her presence at the conference extremely irritating.

Meanwhile the Communist forces were keeping the Japanese tied down in many areas and more and more people, dismayed by the central government's policies, were being recruited by the Communists. Corruption, hoarding, a fast deteriorating economy, lack of loyalty in the army ranks, and Chiang's growing ruthlessness and insensitivity to the needs of his people, were weakening his power in the country. But the U.S., increasingly concerned about the threat of Communism, stepped up its help in spite of warnings from Americans who had a better grasp of the situation in China.

These discerning advisers when they warned of blackmail, gangsters, diversion of lend-lease to personal fortunes, and unimaginable corruption, suffered reproofs and often ignominious dismissals and the U. S. continued its support of the China of the Soongs and their cohorts.

Meanwhile the Soong dynasty was beginning to crumble with Mei-ling and Ai-ling accusing their brother T.V. of acquiring enormous wealth as he built a fortune for himself living in the States and managing deals. There was a suggestion that Ai-ling was at the bottom of a plot to overthrow the government, and Mei-ling was struggling with her health and a disintegrating marriage. Chiang was seeing his former attractive young wife. Meiling was living with the Kungs and now rarely accompanied her husband at public functions. In 1944 she and her sister Ai-ling left China for Brazil where Mei-ling sought medical advice and Ai-ling had dealings with the Brazilian dictator and undoubtedly transferred some of the family fortune to the relative safety of South America.

The two sisters then flew to New York where Mei-ling again underwent medical treatment. At this point a newspaper report announced that she had separated from her husband, that Chiang was living with his former wife and son, but that there would be no divorce for fear of repercussions damaging to China. After a year's absence the two women returned in 1945, but Chiang was primarily interested in his old flames and in the underworld gangs that had supported him in the early days. Mei-ling, not to be outdone, flew back to Chungking and resumed her place as Chiang's partner in power.

In 1948 Chiang sent Mei-ling to Washington to plead for more military and financial assistance to prevent the Communists from taking over. The States again came to Chiang's aid, but Mei-ling was not welcome at the White House or in Congress, and she was considered an embarrassment to the government.

Meanwhile the Red Army was sweeping victoriously over the countryside and Chiang's reign was clearly at an end. He resigned as President of China on January 21, 1949, and bribing the directors of the banks to open their vaults, he absconded with their money and the government's gold reserves, and seizing untold treasures from museums and palaces, left for Taiwan on a gunboat in May. All the members of the Soong family except for Ching-ling left China, the Kungs with a modest one billion dollars U.S. deposited safely outside the country.

Once her husband was established in Taiwan, Mei-ling joined him in January 1950. To the dismay of the Taiwanese their island had been taken from Japan by the allies and turned over to Chiang. They submitted only under threat and suffered massacres and executions before Chiang firmly established himself as the ruler of Taiwan.

In the U.S. Ai-ling, H. H. Kung and T.V. Soong became the liaison team between the States and Taiwan as the U.S. considered Taiwan the bastion of anti-communism. To strengthen the ties Mei-ling flew to the States for several months at the end of 1952 and on her return lavishly hosted American official visitors in Taipei, capital of Taiwan.

In 1952 the U. N. was considering giving a seat to the People's Republic of China. Mei-ling set out for Washington to stir up opposition to this action. On her return to Taiwan she was not received with the due pomp and ceremony she deemed worthy of her position, nor was she met by her husband who was now almost senile. It was obvious that she no longer commanded the respect or support of the Taiwanese, but she hung on as long as possible. Finally in 1959 she went off in a huff to the States where she stayed for well over a year, finally returning to Taiwan for a six year stay. But again in 1965 she went back to Washington to a bit more favourable atmosphere when the Taiwanese Nationalist Embassy entertained lavishly in her honour. But the reason behind this extraordinary display of hospitality was the desire of the Nationalists to secure American support for an invasion of the China mainland whilst the Americans were hoping for Chinese support in Vietnam. But negotiations were useless. Neither side would agree.

Mei-ling decided to settle in Manhattan. Her health was failing, she was sixty-nine years of age and it was discovered that she had cancer. When Chiang died in 1975 she went into permanent exile and lost forever her place as one of the Ten Most Famous Women in contemporary life. Her two older sisters had died, Ai-ling in 1973 and Ching ling in 1981, her brother-in-law H. H. Kung in 1967, a younger brother in 1969, and her famous older brother always known as TV in 1971. However, by late 1999 it was announced that Mei-ling had celebrated her one hundred and first birthday and in the year 2000 this extraordinary woman celebrates her 103rd birthday and publicly comments on the spring elections in Taiwan.

SUMMARY: The Chinese have a saying: "Ai-ling loved money, Mei-ling loved power, Ching-ling loved China." While sweeping generalities are not always accurate in detail, there is no doubt that Ai-ling's financial cunning was notorious, that Mei-ling's power was evidenced in her influence over events both in China and abroad, and that Ching-ling broke with her family to remain loyal to the principles that had guided her and her husband through the years. Whatever the verdict, the lives of the Soong Sisters live on in the annals of modern China.

Chapter 13

Rebellious Youth
Jiang Qing (Madame Mao-Tse-Tung)

Jiang Quing in her early days

Jiang Qing, alias Shumeng, alias Yunhe, alias Lan Ping, was the product of a broken and turbulent home and a broken and tormented country. She was born in March 1914 in a village in Shandong, one of the first provinces to experience foreign imperialism, with the ceding of some areas to France in 1860, the leasing of ports to Britain in 1898, and later the take-over of her province by Germany as a sphere of influence. The year that she was born saw Japan appropriate the German area and she suffered through the consequent instability and bloody confrontations that followed. She saw local citizens decapitated and their heads displayed as a warning to would-be protestors. She saw peasants' crops plundered and people shot at random. As the imperial dynasty had been overthrown in 1911, warlordism was running rampant and the country was in utter chaos. The violence and brutality left its mark on her. She learned to resist attempts to browbeat her or to have other's views imposed on her.

Named Shumeng at birth, she was the daughter of a sixty year old man with a reasonable income from a trade and an inn, but he was a heavy drinker with a poor reputation in the town. Her mother was his concubine and thirty years his junior. To indicate his disgust at the birth of a daughter, her father nicknamed her "Little Mistake". She was treated with contempt by the Number One Wife, and frequently beaten by her father and older half-sister. Her feet were bound as was the custom of the day, but she tore off the bandages and refused to conform. Finally, when her father in a fit of rage took a spade and beat Shunmeng's mother, breaking her hand, the mother strapped Shunmeng on her back and fled.

To make a living the mother went from household to household as a domestic servant, exploited by the men of the family for whom she worked. Eventually the two ended up at the home of the mother's parents in the city of Jinan and the child was sent to primary school. Her name was changed to Yunhe, a flowery name given her by her grandfather but not well suited to the quick-tempered, undisciplined child who had been forced to depend on herself and to outwit those who tried to control her. Her unconforming behaviour led to abuse from teachers and students, and she was finally expelled for fighting. At this point she vowed never to permit anyone to bully her and it became her life-long resolution.

Yunhe's mother seems to have left her daughter, possibly to remarry, when the girl was in her early teens. Yunhe, confused and lonely, began to seek satisfaction for her restless spirit. In a local dance and operatic troupe she found the excitement she craved and the lack of restrictions and conformity that she abhorred. But she also found that once again she was maltreated, and when her grandparents finally discovered her whereabouts and offered to take her back into their household, she reluctantly agreed.

It was not easy for a girl to secure a place in a middle school, and Yunhe rebelled at the idea of returning to a conventional school. It was 1928 and China was in a ferment. Japan was making inroads into north China, Communist ideas were gaining a foothold, strikes and conflicts tore cities apart, and students returning from studies abroad were introducing new ideas to those who were rebelling against the deplorable state of the country.

When her grandparents suggested that it was time to arrange a marriage for her, Yunhe determined to find a way out of her dilemma. She heard about an Experimental Arts Academy that offered an opportunity for young people to study music, art and drama, and since the Academy was financed by the Shandong Department of Education and offered free board, lodging, tuition and a small monthly allowance to its students, Yunhe decided to apply.

To her surprise she was accepted, largely because of her long, flowing hair which was suited to a special role. But once admitted, she cut off her hair and adopted a modern style, and consequently did not qualify for the roles for which she had been intended. However, because of the shortage of women, she was retained and began to work hard, studying dramatic literature, learning to sing traditional opera, and attempting to play the piano. But she was the youngest in the class and her poor clothes and provincial dialect led once again to bullying and reproach.

Finally Yunhe was given a part in a play which she performed with some success, but the school was shortly afterwards shut down by a warlord who overran the city. She joined some of the students and teachers who set up a travelling theatrical group which eventually wound up in Peking in 1930. Yunhe was only 16 years of age, without adequate clothing or bedding, and because of her provincialism and lack of understanding of Peking audiences and style, she was not successful. She realized she lacked advanced education and without the security of a family to fall back on, she was more than ever determined to succeed on her own initiative. She returned to Jinan and accepted the offer of marriage from an older man who had seen her on stage and had liked her performance. But Yunhe could not accept the life of a married woman and the lowly place she held in the family hierarchy. Tempers flared and eventually a friend of hers bargained with the husband for a divorce, a frowned-upon proceeding in those days. The chagrin of her grandparents cut her off entirely from her family.

Yunhe longed to go to Shanghai but without money and contacts such a move was impossible. However, she purchased a train ticket for the nearby city of Qingdao where she knew one of the former directors of the Arts Academy who was now Dean of the new university. Qingdao was a more progressive city with stirrings of the new socialist teachings and strong opposition to the Japanese aggression. But the Dean was not sympathetic to Yunhe and simply offered her temporary shelter in a dormitory. Pitying the young girl's plight, the Dean's wife managed to secure for her a minor position as a clerk in the library. As such, Yunhe had the right to audit classes, many of which were taught by professors who had returned from the United States and were opening up modern ideas to the zealous students. Although warned against trouble-making, Yunhe decided to join the League of Left-Wing Dramatists, a Communist front organization whose purpose was to take propaganda plays to villages, schools and factories. It was a dangerous game as the government agents were always on the lookout for subversive elements, but as the audiences began to support the cast, more and more political ideas were introduced in their presentations.

As Yunhe audited classes, studied literature, and attempted to write some plays, she became more and more aware of the differing ideologies in the political realms. She decided that intellectual pursuits were not as important as actively laying the foundations for revolution. She joined various left wing groups and finally applied for membership in the Communist Party. But it was not until the following spring that she was able to penetrate the secrecy of the party organization in Qingdao and be inducted as a member.

At this time Shanghai was attracting thousands of left-wing writers, artists and dramatists. Yunhe, convinced that that was where she must go, sailed down the coast and landed in that city. But Shanghai was suffering from purges, terrorist tactics and secret agents. It was not easy to make contact with fellow travellers. Her membership in the Qingdao Communist Party did not give her access to the Shanghai branch, and she had some close calls with spies and military police. When she was finally admitted for an interview she was asked what she would do for the party. She offered to do "mass work at the grassroots level" and was finally assigned to a drama group concerned with educational philosophy and social concerns. She began auditing classes at Shanghai University but found it extremely hard to make friends or become involved.

Demonstrations were the order of the day but no forewarning was possible. A sudden message would come of a protest. Supporters then arrived quickly, displayed slogans, issued demands and as quickly disappeared before the authorities could nab them. Every rally was at the risk of a demonstrator's life. Yunhe was frightened by the fate of student radicals but she persisted in her support. Actors frequently left by back stage doors to evade police, and more than once Yunhe ran through back alleys to avoid arrest. She was supporting herself by teaching Chinese in a middle school, but when she received a warning to flee Shanghai she went, in 1932, to Peking and began auditing lectures on political science. She existed on bread and water and spent much of her time in the municipal library reading extensively.

In the spring of 1933, however, she returned to Shanghai. By this time many of the schools were in the hands of the Communist Party and she was assigned to teach in a night school program for women workers. As this particular educational program was directed by the YWCA, Yunhe's position was more secure. The ruling Nationalist Party, eager to have the support of the West, allowed the YM and YW to organize services for the working classes, and since the foreigners were also sympathetic to the boycott of Japanese goods, their patriotic activities were acceptable. Under the aegis of the Y, Yunhe was able to investigate working conditions in the factories, arrange lectures and discussions and produce anti-Japanese plays.

Factory managers, however, were not sympathetic to her activities and she was often faced with obstruction and abuse. She discovered the hellish conditions under which people worked and the exploitation they suffered. Recruits for the factories were drawn from ignorant, poverty-stricken peasants, and children were bought and sold, rationed for food and water and many died. The Nationalist party was not pleased with her work and continually harassed her. Eventually she was kidnapped. Before her captors could search her, she chewed up the application form for membership in the Communist Party that she had in her pocket, but was taken to the police station and locked up for eight months. Finally a girl who was being released from prison was persuaded to contact the YW and with the arrival of a foreigner, the police released Yunhe.

Yunhe then returned to her acting career. Writers were struggling to arouse the masses, but actors were lumped with criminals, prostitutes and vagrants. She attained some success and her popularity increased, but her outspoken criticism of players who, she felt, were prostituting the new nationalism, led to her being threatened.

To add to her dilemma, the Acting Director was pursuing her and finally proposed a sexual relationship. But Yunhe loathed him and flatly refused his offer. As he was a prominent member of the Communist Party he spread false rumours about her and persuaded the left-wing Dramatists league to have nothing more to do with her.

The Communist Party in Shanghai was urban based and followed the lead of Moscow. Mao Tse-tung had split with the Shanghai branch and had fled to the mountains where he was building an army. In 1935 with the rise of Hitler and Mussolini, the active aggression of Japan, and harassment by Chiang Kai-shek and the Nationalist forces, Mao and his Red Army began the Long March that finally led to Yenan where he set up his headquarters.

Shanghai communists were torn by rivalry and defections, and members of drama groups often became traitors or special agents.

Yunhe felt betrayed and friendless but went to live with a theatrical friend in safer quarters in the French concession in Shanghai. She decided to remold her life and chose another name for herself, Lan Ping (blue apple). Blue was her favourite colour and apples reminded her of the fruit of her home province. At twenty years of age, a new personality, Lan Ping, emerged on the Shanghai scene.

She was not a traditional Chinese beauty but neither was she an unattractive woman. Five feet five in height, she was slim, small-boned and lithesome. Like many Chinese women she had graceful hands which she used well for artistic expression. She loved to dance and when dressed in the modish style of the day, the long straight gown with the slit sides, and with her flashing smile and grace she was able to attract the attention of men.

To her delight Lan Ping was given the part of Nora in Ibsen's play The Doll House, and interpreted the heroine as a convincing rebel, a liberated woman. Her success led in 1937 to a film contract but she was often expected to be the plaything of the director to whom she owed her position. She resented the power of the men in the entertainment world and determined not to allow herself to be possessed or bullied by anyone. Over the years she had been briefly married twice and undoubtedly slept with lovers as was the fashion in the seething, decadent life of Shanghai, but her impulsiveness, her boldness, her inability to work with a team, her determination not to be controlled by anyone, made it almost impossible for her to form lasting attachments, much less accept the usual role of a Chinese wife. But that very impulsiveness and the passion with which she expressed herself did help to make her performances on stage and in film successful.

But political issues were soon to disrupt the course of stage and screen in Shanghai. Japan began her campaign against China in the summer of 1937, and within weeks Shanghai fell to the enemy. Lan Ping could not remain in Shanghai with any degree of safety. Her growing ambition, her struggle to assert herself, her refusal to be confined by any traditional bonds forced her to reassess her life and to yearn for greater control over events that shaped her future. In Yenan where Mao Tse-tung had his headquarters she saw an opportunity not only in the dramatic field but also the possibility of working with the Communist political movement. So Lan Ping, at the age of 23, set her sights on the Communist stronghold of Yenan in the hills of northwest China.

Yenan

Chapter 19

Jiang Qing's Revenge
Madame Mao-Tse-Tung (Part 2)

Jiang Quing at her trial

Yenan was an organized socialist community made up of the survivors of the Long March who had crossed eighteen mountain ranges and twenty-four rivers to take refuge in the mountain caves around Yenan. The army became self-sufficient and gave local peasants assistance with their crops and harvest. A new society emerged in the area with the farmer as the core, and there developed a loyalty to Mao that resisted all fabulous bribes from the Nationalists for Mao dead or alive. It was into this venue that Lan Ping headed.

Fortunately she had a contact in Yenan with one of her friends from school days, but the journey to the remote settlement posed many problems. She set out from Xian as the launching point purely on spec, certain that something would turn up. Luckily in Xian she met Madame Xu who had schooled her in politics in Shanghai. Together the two women passed the days together waiting for endorsement to continue their journey. Finally the permits arrived and they set off with a group in an army truck. But storms raged in the mountains and the road was washed out. Local farmers offered some of the marooned refugees a few scrawny horses. Lan Ping had never ridden a horse in her life but when she mounted and the animal would not move she cut a willow switch and applied it vigorously. The horse took off in a wild gallop until it became exhausted, leaving Lan Ping stranded. Eventually Xu and the wagon party managed to get through, caught up with her and all arrived in Luochan where the Communist leadership were meting to develop strategy.

Xu's husband, one of the participants at the meeting, arranged for the assorted hitch-hikers to ride the fifty miles to Yenan in the back of a truck. When Mao Tse-tung emerged to join the convoy it was Lan Ping's first glimpse of the powerful leader and she suddenly felt her youthfulness, her lack of political qualifications and her own incompetence. She was aware that it was a male society of hardened revolutionaries seasoned by the incredible hardships of the Long March. But she was determined to make her mark in spite of her political naivete. Her political past was not one to inspire the authorities but she decided that her Shanghai poise and her ability to attract men were her chief assets.

Some of her former associates now resident in Yenan testified against her, but eventually she was accepted for the Party School, one of a small minority of women among hundreds of men. With the establishment of a film studio she hoped to pursue her career in drama, but she was not considered a good actress and was not acclaimed by audiences that saw her on stage. She was fortunate, however, to find an old friend from her days in Shandong who sponsored her application to enter Lu Shun College which had been set up in Yenan. She was accepted as a student and teaching assistant, although she resented the fact that she was dependent on a man's favour and not on her own merit for her position.

At this time Mao was living alone in his cave home. His marital experiences had all ended in disaster. His first arranged marriage to a peasant girl in his home village had not been consummated. His second wife was the liberated daughter of one of his teachers in the city of Changsha. She bore him three sons but was beheaded in 1930 by the Hunan warlord because she refused to denounce her husband and the Communist party.

Mao's third wife, He Zizhen, who had accompanied him on the Long March, was unable to cope with the situation in Yenan. She fled the city but returned in 1937. Ill and worn out from the Long March and the birth of five children in seven years, she was physically and mentally exhausted. Their relationship that had been forged in the strenuous days of the Long

March came apart in 1937, aided and abetted by jealousy over Mao's liaison with a glamorous young actress named Lily Wu. He Zizhen was finally sent by the Party to the Soviet Union for medical attention.

By way of diversion the leaders mingled with the populace at informal dances, to the music of scratchy western records or locally organized Chinese orchestras. Long March survivors would dance a two step or waltz with a bright young student from the local university, and tractor mechanics would swing the wives of Politburo notables.

Mao continued to live alone for some time until by chance he met Lan Ping when he visited the College. She took the opportunity after his address to attract his attention with some questions. For Mao the arts were important as a tool in the revolution and he had begun to foresee the value of music and drama in the educational campaign. Over the weeks the unsung but attractive twenty-four year old actress, Lan Ping, and the powerful forty-five year old leader met on occasions, sometimes at visits in his cave quarters and occasionally on clandestine meetings. Lan Ping and Mao began sleeping together

Sympathy for He Zizhen and resentment towards the promiscuous Shanghai actress caused a furor in the community. Lan Ping's friend, Kang from Shandong who had now become a part of Mao's inner committee, decided a solution had to be found. When it was discovered that Lan Ping was pregnant, the leaders finally agreed to a divorce for Mao, and in late 1938 Lan Ping and Mao were officially married. But Lan Ping had a price to pay. She was forbidden to assume any political role. This restriction built up within her a smouldering resentment that exploded a decade later. For the time being, however, she accepted her dependence as Mao's housewife, but continued to harbour secret aspirations to express herself and be an independent person in her own right.

At this point Lan Ping and Mao decided that a new name was in order and they chose Jiang Qing. Jiang (river) and Qing (green) had numerous implications and the sound was effective. Jiang Qing learned to shop and cook and developed an avid predilection for bridge, which was highly popular with the party leaders. Finally she gave birth to a daughter. Although both she and Mao had each been married several times, it was her first child, but for Mao his ninth. Because of the exigencies of the times many of Mao's offspring had been given to peasant families to raise, but some of them were reintroduced into the family and became Jiang Qing's responsibility.

As time passed Jiang Qing began to assert herself, participating in party discussions, and when possible rewarding friends and denouncing enemies. She began to advise Mao on decisions, although both being self-opinionated and head-strong, quarrels were not infrequent. By taking over as Mao's secretary she became party to his plans and familiar with his correspondence.

At this time foreign visitors to the Communist headquarters in Yenan spoke of her as an attractive woman, a good bridge player, and an excellent cook. Although she now suffered from TB she continued to teach dramatic arts at the Lu Hsun Academy and directed anti-Japanese propaganda plays for use in the countryside. Her illness was used as a ploy by others to limit her public appearances, but those from abroad who met her spoke of her vitality and good health.

Once the war with Japan ended in 1945, the War of Liberation became intense. Military strategy was in the hands of his generals while Mao pursued his role of political theorist. His writings were published and spread throughout the nation as the liberation forces progressed. In March 1947 an air attack by the Nationalists on Yenan disrupted the community. A mass exodus began and Jiang Qing and her daughter, Li Na, were the only women left in the cave homes of Yenan. Finally Mao, his entourage and a detachment of the Red Army set out at night on a perilous journey. The Nationalist army had devastated much of the territory through which they passed, but as they went Jiang Qing lectured soldiers and local people on the aims and goals of the Communist Party. The Party won the support of the populace by restoring order, freeing those unjustly jailed, and helping the farmers bring in what harvest had not been appropriated by the Nationalists.

Throughout 1947-48 the Red Army with Mao and Jiang Qing survived bomb attacks and deprivation, carried out land reform and built a base of support along the way, with Mao continuing to write on basic rules for a free society. Finally in April 1949 the Red Army marched on Nanking and Shanghai, and by October 1, 1949, Mao stood on the steps of the Forbidden City in Beijing and proclaimed the People's Republic of China.

Jiang Qing was nowhere to be seen in all the ceremonies. After two years on the march she weighed 92 pounds, had a persistent fever, and was completely devoid of energy. She was sent to Yalta on the Black Sea for care and convalescence, but returned after a couple of months determined to tour the countryside in support of land reform. Mao opposed her plan but she persisted and set off for Shanghai. Prevented from appearing there, she went on to Wusih which had been disastrously devastated by the Japanese. Here she appealed to the women to take their place in the revolution, and gradually she became recognized as Mao's wife.

With the outbreak of the Korean War, anger at the U. S. rose to fever pitch, and when one of Mao's sons was killed in battle both Mao and Jiang Qing were deeply affected. In January 1951 they left for a respite in the south where Mao did some more writing and began to preview films for distribution. Jiang Qing became a self-appointed censor and particularly denounced the foreign films that promoted capitalism and foreign values. Before long she was appointed Director of the Cinema Department, and she set out to use the arts to change attitudes and mould thought. However, because of her health she moved back and forth from China to Russia, always fearing she might be kept as a hostage, interned in a mental hospital, or discarded for another wife. Few people in China knew her, she had little power and was only able to exercise what little influence she had through her husband. Influential leaders, determined to be rid of her, saw that she was sent again to Moscow for treatment where she remained from the winter of '52 to the fall of '53. Finding little relief for her illness and sensing the strained relations between China and Russia, she returned home but was bedridden for much of the time till the end of 1958. During this period she read widely, focused on the doctrine of struggle between the working class and the bourgeoisie, and occasionally prepared reports and did investigative work for Mao.

In 1955 a gifted writer, Hu Feng, attacked the party for its attitude to the arts. In reply Mao issued his famous speech "Let a Hundred Flowers Blossom, Let a Hundred Schools of Thought Contend." But this proclamation let loose a flood of criticism against the Party. Mao's answer was another publication "On the Correct Handling of Contradictions Among The People." Posters went up everywhere. Debates and arguments flourished. At this point Jang Qing fell seriously ill and a gynecologist diagnosed cervical cancer. For the fourth time she was sent to Moscow. Ill and depressed she wondered if she had reached the end of the road.

But her astonishing will power, her craving for success and an amazingly rigorous program of exercise restored her health and in 1962 she returned, seemingly fully recovered and eager to delve once more into the cultural field. She persuaded Mao that he should promote the proletarian arts and he began to insist that to narrow the differences between urban and rural life, singers and writers should go to the countryside to learn from those at the grassroots. Jiang Qing intensified her criticism of all drama that was based on the past and was not in accord with class struggle and emerging socialist ideals. Mao supported his wife and called for a ban on all plays featuring royal personages, spirits, outstanding scholars, or women whose only claim to stardom was beauty and sex appeal. Controversy raged when some leading artists suggested that plays of the past had artistic qualities not found in the new operas and plays.

Jiang Qing's opportunity came when she was invited to write an article on the revolution in Peking Opera as an introduction to a unique Festival of Peking Opera on Contemporary Themes held in the summer of 1964. The festival was important because of the large number of people involved and for the emphasis on bringing the performing arts into line with the politics of New China. Jiang Qing gave the opening speech in which she spoke of the need to portray the peasants and workers who were the life blood of the new society and the soldiers who were the protectors of the motherland. But she was frustrated when her appeal for a troupe to carry out these ideas was refused.

To help her gain her ends she made an agreement with Lin Piao, an army commander and hero of the Long March. She obtained a position in the top echelon of the army and was now in touch with the Forum on Work in Literature and Art in the Armed Forces. Wearing army fatigues, she addressed a mass meeting of soldiers urging them to take up pen, brush, camera or musical instrument and celebrate the army's revolutionary successes by creating works of literature and art. She then assembled writers, actors, singers and dancers in an attempt to remould the arts.

She and Mao then began to plan. Both had been concerned about the growing number of educated young people who had had no experience in the war of resistance or had not lived in the pre-revolutionary era. Where did their loyalty lie? Mao, now sixty five and suffering from Parkinson's disease, became more open to Jiang Qing whose strong will had often angered him but now appeared as an extension of his own determination. She made a survey of trends on University campuses and began to mobilize the youth under the banner of Mao Tse-tung Thought and a destruction of the four olds (old culture, old ideology, old customs and old habits.)

The summer and fall of 1966 was a period of tremendous unrest.

Millions of students were invited to leave their schools and homes and on foot, bicycle, truck or train to rally in Beijing. Wearing red scarves these young people, now known as the Red Guards, massed in Tiananamen Square. Jiang Qing in her glory addressed them, beginning her remarks with the words, "I have been asked by Chairman Mao to send you his regards." After she had built up a mass hysteria, Mao appeared accompanied by Lin Piao, with Jiang Qing standing nearby looking glamorous and excited.

In the following months Jiang Qing appeared at other massive rallies or in motorcades, her constant theme being the denunciation of plays that featured characters reminiscent of the decadent past. The performing arts were made subject to the jurisdiction of the Cultural Revolution Committee. Now in the seat of power, Jiang Qing began to settle old scores. Those who had opposed her, had thwarted her in the old days in Shanghai, who did not support her use of art for the revolution were the victims of her revenge. They were ridiculed, hounded, lost their jobs and were driven to despair and often to suicide. Those who dared to question her background found themselves in prison and their associates suspect. The media came under the control of the Cultural Committee and newspapers, journals and books that did not toe the line were discontinued.

With the growing unrest and chaos Mao began to weaken his support but to stabilize the situation there grew up a Mao cult. Mao was pictured as the radiant sun, his little red book became the bible of the revolution, and Jiang Qing basked in the radiance. But the movement took a violent turn and fighting broke out between rival factions. Lin Piao with the power of the army behind him controlled mass behaviour and public presentations.

As Mao's health deteriorated Jiang Qing became concerned about her place in history. Was she merely Mao's wife or a leader in her own right whose power would continue when Mao died? Lin Piao, Jiang Qing's rival for the leadership, set out on a vacation flight but strangely two hours later the plane crashed and all aboard were killed. Jiang Qing began to see herself as a modern Empress Wu whose unique place in Chinese history as the only female ruler, inspired her to study the history and career of this conniving woman. She saw her own quest for power as a revolt akin to that of the dispossessed of her country battling the ignominy and degradation of the past. Mao deplored her actions but did little to curb them. He retired from Beijing and with his departure from the centre of power, Jiang Qing held sway, making appointments that would work in her favour but always inferring that what she did was according to oral orders from Mao.

Intrigue and undercurrents were rampant and when Mao died on Sept 5, 1976, Jiang Qing was in a panic as to what her place would be in the new era. She did not mourn her husband as a widow, but, as she wrote on his funeral wreath, as "your student and comrade in arms."

The Government at this time had little power. Each rival group was planning a coup d'etat. On the evening of October 6, a squad of motorcycles and a military jeep manned by troops quietly entered the grounds of Jiang Qing's villa and burst into her bedroom. "You are under arrest", they said as they pointed their guns at a ferocious woman. Her enemies had succeeded and she and her cohorts were brought to trial.

During the trial in 1980 Jiang Qing refused to confess to any misdemeanours. The whole world watched on TV as she and the three men who were most closely associated with her, commonly know as the Gang of Four, were put on trial. Ever the actress, she groomed herself for the occasion and exploited every moment before a vast audience. Her crimes were listed as two fold, the persecution and destruction of intellectuals and any who opposed her, and her attempt to take over the powers of state.

Calmly defiant, Jiang Qing refuted their claims until worn down by session after session she became belligerent, yet always aware of her dramatic role to the reluctant admiration of those who watched her performance nightly on TV. Many young people used to passive acceptance admired her spirited defence and her display of self-will. Many felt that it was not her wrong ideas but her defiance of the correct code of a woman in Chinese society that was her undoing.

When the final verdict was announced it was an ambivalent sentence, death, but suspended for two years to give her a chance to rectify her thought. It was a verdict that avoided making her a martyr and in some ways passed judgement on Mao himself.

When in 1983 the two year suspension was ended, the Party investigated the situation. She had not repented but she had not resisted her detention in any aggressive way. The decision was made that she should remain in jail indefinitely. For eight years little was heard of her until in 1991 there was an announcement that barely caused a ripple. Jiang Qing had committed suicide, her final declaration that she alone controlled her life and her death.

Chapter 15

Beloved Author and Social Conscience
Bing Xin (1900-1999)

Bing Xin and her cat

Whenever I mentioned to anyone, Chinese or Westerner, that I was to have an interview with Bing Xin they would look at me in awed surprise. So revered was Madame Bing Xin that people spoke of her in hushed tones.

"Just five minutes," I was told by those who arranged the interview. "Time to bring greetings and take a picture. She's 91 and has had a stroke and broken her hip."

I expected to find a frail invalid with whom it would be difficult to communicate. Instead, I found an alert woman, sitting at her desk and ready to talk. It was true that she could not move with ease, but her mind was still active and lively. Having graduated from Wellesley College in the United States and travelled extensively throughout the world, Madame Bing Xin spoke English fluently, which made our talk together so much more intimate and meaningful.

My Chinese friends who had arranged the interview said that the customary gift should be a copy of my recently published book *I Saw Three Chinas*. When I offered it to Madame Bing Xin she immediately said, "I'll certainly read this." According to her friends she reads books and newspapers for 7 to 8 hours a day, following current events and important issues with great interest. She began to turn the pages of my book and when she came to the photos she started to ask questions. Nothing would do but I must sit beside her and tell her about them.

Madame Bing Xin's daughter, Wu Bing, was present and she added to the conversation. She was an active member of the Beijing City Council, known for her radical and aggressive approach. She is fluent in English and later gave me further details of her mother's life and work.

As Madame Bing Xin and I talked, a large white cat walked across the desk and sat in front of us, demanding attention. Madame Bing Xin laughed and explained that Mimi was her constant companion and was expecting a treat. Mimi's nose was probing the top drawer. Madame opened it and to Mimi's delight produced a Whiskas titbit. I was amused to find American Whiskas in a Beijing drawer.

My guide who had accompanied me was busy snapping pictures, but Madame said,

"I'll give you a picture of me and the cat that was taken recently," and she drew a lovely snapshot from her drawer, signed it on the back and handed it to me.

A half hour had passed in her company, a wonderful half hour with this charming woman whose life had been so inextricably tied up with her country's history for nearly a century. Looking through my book she had remarked:

"There's only nine years difference in our ages. We have both seen great changes in China, haven't we?"

I was honoured to be in her presence and to have the opportunity to talk to someone so beloved and revered by her people.

Bing Xin was born in Fuzhou City in Fujian province on October 5, 1900. Her given name was Xie Wang Ying, but she assumed the pen name of Bing Xin when she began to write. Her father was an officer in the Chinese navy with a great love for his country, and he obviously imparted that love to his daughter. She was also an omnivorous reader, tackling ancient novels at the age of seven.

Bing Xin spent her childhood at Yantai, on Bohai Bay off the coast of Shandong province. She was a lonely child and the ocean became to her a source of wonder.

Colourful mornings and evenings beside the water stimulated her imagination and gave her insight as a poet. She wrote many fragmentary thoughts in her notebook and several years later her brothers encouraged her to have the stanzas printed and they appeared under the title A Maze of Stars.

When the Sun Yat Sen Revolution of 1911 rocked the nation, Bing Xin was attending classes for female students at Fuzhou College. However, in 1913 her family moved to Beijing and the following year she began her studies at a church high school for girls. Her desire to become a medical doctor led her in 1918 to preparatory classes run by an American Mission University. It was at this time that the most important event of her life transformed her from a medical student to a writer.

In May 1919 the Chinese delegation to the signing of the Versailles peace treaty was ignominiously treated. China's demands were ignored and students in Beijing were furious. They persuaded their fellow countrymen studying in Paris to picket the hotel where the Chinese delegation was staying to prevent them from attending the ratification ceremony. In Beijing a mass protest inaugurated the May 4 movement which awakened a national fervour that has had a permanent effect. Bing Xin, still known by her name Xie Wan Ying, worked as a secretary for the student organization and began to publish articles in the Beijing morning newspaper.

Her appetite whetted, she started to look at the many social problems facing the China of her day, and in September of 1919, under the pen name of Bing Xin, she produced her first novel. "It was the May 4 Movement that led me to a writing career," she asserts.

She went out on the streets to raise money and to urge people to support the May 4 Movement, while her evenings were devoted to her writing. But she continued her studies and in 1921 began undergraduate work at Xie He University where she met famous writers and became involved in a literary research association. She attempted a novel about Chinese youth with the intention of helping them in their search for meaning in their lives, but she was unable to resolve the problem at that time. Instead she portrayed a story about the love of a mother for her son, developing the idea of love which became very much a part of her lifelong philosophy. She was able to combine traditional Chinese literature with western style, which made her very popular with the young people of the day.

Influenced by the Indian poet, Rabindranath Tagore, she also experimented with some very beautiful short poems. The following, translated by two Professors of English, is a charming example of her poetry.

STARS
Stars, millions of stars gleam in the endless dark blue.
What man has ever listened to their distant dialogue?
In silence, in weak light,
They acclaim one another with untiring zeal.[5]

By 1923 she was able to publish a collection of stories under the title of Superman, and two collections of poems, Myriads of Stars, and Spring River. At the same time she graduated from university with the Golden Key award for top marks.

Her excellence was rewarded with a scholarship to the renowned Wellesley College in Massachusetts State, U.S.A. In August of 1923 she set sail for America. On board were two famous Chinese writers and a young man named Wu Wen Zhao who was on his way to take up studies in sociology and ethnology. He was critical of Bing Xin's writing, claiming that she did not have enough background and knowledge to express herself. Bing Xin was impressed with his learning and open-mindedness and during the course of their discussions the two young people fell in love. They were destined for different universities but through correspondence and occasional meetings at holiday resorts their friendship blossomed. He admired her ability to combine new thought with traditional ethics, and his love for her grew.

In 1926 when Bing Xin received her MA from Wellesley College, Wu Wen Zhao proposed. "I wish to write to your parents and ask for permission to marry you," he said, so together they wrote a 3,000 word letter to her parents which was signed only by the young man. Bing Xin carried this letter back to China with her and when her parents read Wu's expressions of love and the meaning of marriage, they were impressed with his sincerity. They readily agreed to the marriage on his return from the States. Meanwhile Bing Xin lectured at several different universities in China.

In 1929 Wu Wen Zhao returned to China and received appointments at two of Beijing's prestigious universities. The following year the happy couple went to Shanghai to visit Bing Xin's parents and to participate in an engagement party. Later that year the marriage ceremony took place at Yen Ching University, a marriage of deep respect and love that lasted for over fifty years until Wu's death in 1985.

When Bing Xin lived in the States she had begun to write stories for children in the form of Letters to Chinese Young Readers, which were published in a Beijing newspaper in a column called Children's World. These letters, published in book form in 1926, spoke of her love for her homeland, rather than descriptions of her life in the West. From 1926 to 1935 this collection was republished twenty-one times, and Bing Xin became the most popular children's writer in the country.

But with the Japanese intrusion into Manchuria, Bing Xin was once again provoked into concern for her country and her people. In her novel Separation she showed her deep concern for the hard life of the workers and her intense feelings for a working woman who could not feed her son although her work provided ample food for the estate owner's son.

When the Japanese invasion of China became out-and-out war, Bing Xin and her husband moved to Kunming in the interior of China. There she became a volunteer teacher in a Normal School in Sichuan province, later moving to Chungking where many of her articles were published in a Weekly Review.

With the defeat of Japan, Bing Xin and her husband went to Japan hoping to restore friendship between the two nations. From 1949-51 she taught a Chinese modern literature course at Tokyo University and published short articles in Japanese newspapers and women's magazines.

Following their sojourn in Japan, Bing Xin and her husband returned to China, but two years later she began to travel extensively, mostly to writer's conferences. First to India, then in 1956 to Russia and Czechoslovakia, in 1958 to France, England, Italy and Switzerland, in 1962 to Egypt, and in 1963 to Africa to attend an African Writers Conference. In between these journeys she was a frequent visitor to Japan, always encouraging friendship between the former enemies.

The Cultural Revolution (1966-76) was a devastating time for the educated class. At 70 years of age Bing Xin was sent to a Cadre School to do physical labour for 14 months, from June 1970 to August 1971. In 1973 Hong Kong publishers were able to publish her book Apple Blossoms and Friendship in which she urged the people of China and Japan to establish friendly relations.

After the fall of the Gang of Four in 1976, her third book of Letters to Children was published, maintaining her reputation as the leading writer for children. But at the same time she was writing essays and translating some of Tagore's works, while her own works were being translated into English, German, Japanese and French, making her an international figure in the literary world.

At 79 years of age she was chosen as Vice-President of the Chinese Literature and Art Association, a tribute to her influence in the literary world. About this time she also began her autobiography which was a powerful and poignant record of the great historical and social changes that had occurred during her lifetime.

In the February 1992 issue of the magazine Women of China, Shu Yi, Director of the Chinese Modern Literature Gallery in Beijing wrote an article entitled "Bing Xin, A Writer with an Outstanding Personality." Describing the celebration of her ninetieth birthday two years previously, he said "Bing Xin clearly states her likes and dislikes, yet has a magical way of dealing with everything in a gentle, cordial and dignified manner. She is still quick witted and has a formidable memory. She discusses everything with a smile, using her own eloquent manner of speech coloured with witty remarks. She is really a special woman."

In spite of her 92 years, Bing Xin was still writing short stories, prose and essays on important issues that touched the lives of the people of her day. One of China's leading writers, Ba Jin, said to her "You are the conscience of Chinese intellectuals." Since 1978 she has written approximately 300 articles and her mind was still alert.

Her chief themes were stories on current affairs and social issues and on the philosophy of love. Her story Superman, ably translated many years ago by Jeff Book, presents the theme she so ardently pursued, the place and power of love in human life. In this story she traced the development of a cynical young man who has no friends. "The world is empty," he says, "and life is in fact an unconscious state. We have nothing in common, we share nothing. It is better to reject each other and get on with life." But as the story progresses the young man, angered by the disturbing moans of a sick boy, pays to have a doctor attend him. Out of this experience and the love of the boy for his benefactor emerges a compassion that changes the direction of the young man's life. Beautifully told, with sentimentality, one sees the evolution of a new approach to life through the simple act that originally was conceived in anger but through love brought the gift of new life. As the young man says to the boy in a final letter, "You used your love to awaken my sleeping soul."

As I sat talking to this charming, incisive woman, I realized that she had nourished three generations of her people. Her life had spanned the most cataclysmic century of China's history and hers was a voice that had spoken and was still speaking to young and old of love and friendship, of social responsibility and pride in their motherland.

China's beloved matriarch lived on to the close of the century still writing and proclaiming her lifelong philosophy until she passed away on February 28, 1999, "with a smile on her lips" as the Chinese newspaper reported. Thus ended the life of one of China's outstanding women who had a decisive impact on the life of her country.

Wu Bing (daughter), the author, Bing Xin

Chapter 16

Innovative Manager
Zhi Mei Wing

Zhi Mei Wing in her apartment

It was a turbulent period when Zhi Mei Wing was born in 1934. Chinese politics were chaotic. Chiang Kai Shek was trying to establish a national government, Mao Tse-tung was gathering his forces in the south preparatory to his Long March to the north-west, and the Japanese were forcing their way further and further into Chinese territory. When Mei Wing was three years old the Japanese finally launched their offensive against China, and Shanghai, Mei Wing's home city, was captured by the Japanese invaders. Her parents moved to Changzhou but before long Japanese forces took over that city also.

In Changzhou Mei Wing managed to attend primary school from which she graduated in 1945. In 1949 Changzhou was liberated by the Chinese Communist army and Zhi Mei Wing joined the party's Youth League while completing her middle school and graduating in 1951.

Mei Wing's father was a railway employee and her mother a stocking factory worker who gave up her job to care for Mei Wing, her two older brothers and a younger sister. With only one income the family of six lived in poverty. Soon after she graduated Mei Wing entered the Eastern China Textile Institute of Shanghai and because of her excellent work she was honoured as one of only two students invited to join the Communist Party.

So successful had she been in her studies that upon graduation from the Institute in 1955 she was offered a teaching position in the Institute, but romance coloured her decision. Wang Wei Jian, a high school classmate, had captured her heart. For a time their paths diverged but they kept in touch. When Wang was appointed to the staff of Xing Hua University in Beijing, Mei Wing managed to secure a position as a specialist in textiles in the Third Textile Mill in Beijing. There, in 1955, began an outstanding career that has lasted till the present day.

But the road was not always easy. In 1958 she was deprived of her membership in the Party and demoted from her job as a technician to that of a manual labourer in the workshop because she insisted on what she considered to be better methods and techniques. But in spite of personal trauma she never relinquished her determination to implement changes and improvements in the textile industry. She became an expert in choosing the best cotton for the various uses of the fabric, studying the areas where cotton was grown and the methods of cultivation best suited to the quality she required

In 1960 at the age of 26 she and Wang Wei were married and two boys were subsequently born.

Meanwhile Mei Wing's ability was so evident that she soon rose to prominence in the Textile Mill and began again to promote change.

Some Chinese have a saying, "if you use more intelligent people than yourself you are defeating yourself." In other words, don't promote people who might supplant you. But Zhi Mei Wing would have none of that. She sought out the best brains in the work force regardless of her own position, but her leadership was such that she remained at the top. "It's easy to recruit a thousand soldiers but hard to find a general," she would say, "but when you find a general you use her, regardless of your own job. It is no good worrying about personal gain. It is the result that counts."

Step by step Zhi Mei Wing rose to the top to become President and Manager of the Third Textile Mill which became one of the leading productive enterprises in the industry. Currently it has 9,800 employees and its production capacity has consistently risen so that it had become one of China's export giants.

"We cannot live two lives", she said. "Once is enough to make our contribution to the world," and contribute she did. From deputy general engineer she took over the position of President when competition in the industry was becoming more and more intense. The Government, evaluating the situation, recommended a ten per cent reduction in cloth production because of the declining market. But the Government didn't reckon with Zhi Mei Wing. In spite of its recommendations she defied the government and set out to make policy changes in order to revive the industry.

During the early 1980's over one thousand of her factory employees quit their jobs to move into the hotel and service industries. Tourism was booming and new hotels were offering many opportunities.

"Let them go," said Zhi. "If they don't want to stay they won't make good workers. We'll attract those who want to work here with new and better methods."

In 1988 Zhi went to Rome on a business trip where she met some of her major customers. West German and British companies advised her that they were about to cut their imports by 20% because of the poor and inconsistent quality and high cost of Chinese products. They warned her that in the end China would lose its current position in the world market because of tough competition from other Asian countries.

Undaunted, Zhi returned to her factory to launch a major battle to maintain China's place in the world markets. She devised what she called the Three A's programme. Ace Standards, Ace Equipment and Ace Belief.

Her first change was to modify 768 of the weaving machines so that the cloth that was produced was 70 inches wide instead of 44. Sales overseas rose dramatically, and most of the 3,000 machines were then modified to meet demand.

She then set out to identify the largest expense items and assess the problems. She discovered that co-ordination of operation was hampered by the late arrival of critical items that slowed the production process and caused the mill to run below its capacity. Chemical components at times were often not available in quantities required and as a result quality suffered. She decided to overstock and was criticized for so doing until the wisdom of her decision was recognized when other mills had to shut down temporarily because of short supply.

Her third major step was to recognize and use research institutions. She carefully co-ordinated joint projects and used innovative methods devised by universities and technical colleges which resulted in greatly improving the quality and consistency of the products her factory produced.

Zhi's energy, foresight and managerial skills paid off. Her products have regained their markets in twenty-five countries and Zhi was cited in a publication of Chinese Women Entrepreneurs as one of the outstanding leaders in the textile industry. Beside being President of the enormous Third Textile Mill she became an Associate Director of Chinese Women Entrepreneurs, sat on the Board of Directors of the Beijing Technological and Managerial Modernization Institute and the Board of the Beijing branch of the China Institute of Textile Engineering, and is a member of the standing committee of the Women's Federation of China.

When I had the privilege of interviewing her in Beijing in 1991, I was overwhelmed by the size of the operation. Our heads covered with white caps to protect our hair from the fine dust, we were guided through what seemed like miles of machines and were given facts about 126,840 spindles, 19,380 thread reels, 3,279 weaving machines with an annual production of 25,000 tons or 95 million metres of cloth. The figures were too overwhelming to grasp, but the visit to this clean, efficient factory with its nearly 10,000 employees was a fascinating and informative experience. Zhi Mei Wing deserved her listing in the book of *Outstanding Women*, published in the early '90's.

inside the cotton mills

Chapter 17

She Makes Clay Live
Zhang Runzi

Zhang Run Zi in her studio

Zhang Runzi was born in 1928 to an impoverished couple in the countryside on the outskirts of the city known today as Dalian. Because of the poverty of her parents she was a scrawny child, small and undernourished. Her mother died when Runzi was only three years old and her father disappeared, leaving the child to be brought up by equally impoverished grandparents.

It was Runzi's task to go shoeless over the hills and streams to the town to pick up bundles of leather scraps, which she brought back to her home. The family then sewed these scraps into larger leather pieces and returned them to the factory in the town to be made into garments.

One day at the age of fourteen Runzi passed a private school. An elderly teacher at the gate of the school was carrying a large bowl of water. As he tried to set it down, Runzi came to his assistance.

"What is your name? To what family do you belong?" asked the teacher

Too shy to answer, Runzi slipped away, but some days later, accompanied by grandmother, she passed the school again. The old teacher was sitting by the gate and inquired of the grandmother what the child's name was. Poor families often did not give names to their children and Runzi was simply called "girl."

"How old is she?" inquired the teacher

"Fourteen," said the grandmother.

The teacher was surprised. "Why is she so small and thin compared to other girls?" he asked.

"We have little food," explained the grandmother

"I will give her a name," said the teacher. "It will be Run Zi, which means "growing up like the grass.""

The teacher wrote the name on a piece of paper but Run Zi wasn't very pleased. The characters were difficult and as she couldn't write she knew they would be too hard for her to copy.

"I'll teach you to read and write," said the teacher.

"That's not possible," said the grandmother. "She has to work and has no time for classes."

"When she comes into town for the leather," said the teacher, "she can come and I will give her a lesson. Then she can take it home and learn it as she walks over the paths and as she sews at home."

Runzi had no money for books or paper but she salvaged scraps of paper thrown away by students and she struggled to learn as best she could.

When she was fifteen years old her grandmother received a letter from Runzi's father asking if his daughter was still alive. He had remarried and wanted the girl to come and live with him. The grandmother was opposed to the move, but the father insisted and Runzi went to the city and became a servant of the stepmother.

Neighbours saw how poor the girl was and advised the stepmother that Runzi ought to go to school. The stepmother finally agreed to allow her to go for two years but at eighteen she must marry. Runzi, then sixteen, began to study in the primary school with eight and nine year olds. Fortunately she had a very kind teacher who had never married and who came to love Runzi as her own child. She took time after class was dismissed to give extra tuition to the girl who had only two years in which to complete her primary education

Runzi, however, studied so hard that she completed her primary education in one year, and prepared to start her middle school work. She qualified to go to the top middle school in the city of Tianjin where she lived, but she had so undermined her constitution that she developed tuberculosis and had to give up school after half a year.

Recovering somewhat from her illness, she was determined to continue her education, but without the means to do so, she scouted around for possibilities. She saw an advertisement for help wanted in a mental hospital, but friends advised her not to apply because she was too small and weak. However, they told her of a private nursing school that paid for food, clothes and board for their pupils. Runzi knew that if she could become independent, her stepmother could not force her into a marriage.

Not particularly interested in nursing, she nevertheless applied, passed the very difficult entrance exams and was accepted as a student. The staff members were very dubious of her ability to cope, but at the end of three years she topped the class of ninety students and was appointed an instructress of nurses. Her health improved and she accepted the position although her heart was not truly in the nursing profession.

Runzi loved to read and craved quiet time to enjoy her books. When other students and staff went out to engage in various activities, she preferred to remain in the dormitory to read and study. Now, at twenty-five years of age, her health had improved to such an extent that a medical examination after graduation proved positive. As she looked ahead she wondered what the years held for her.

A year later she met Su Zhenwu, a teacher at Chinghua University in Beijing who was visiting his parents in Tianjin. The pair fell in love and before long they were married and Runzi went to live in Beijing.

The demands of her work and study however, had taken their toll and at twenty-seven Runzi's tuberculosis returned. She found herself in hospital with a depressing prognostication from the doctors. Her husband who loved her dearly was grieved that his salary was inadequate to cover the expensive medicines that the doctors prescribed and Runzi herself was unable to work. She longed for a child but pregnancy was out of the question. However her brother, father of four girls, offered to let Runzi have one of his little ones on condition that if Runzi died, as was expected, the child would be returned to her parents. There grew up between the foster mother and the child a warm love that sustained and encouraged Runzi in her fight to regain her health.

Runzi transferred to a traditional medicine hospital in the hope that there she might find relief. One day when she was lying on her sick bed her little foster daughter came to see her.

"Why have you come with those dirty hands?" Runzi asked.

The little girl produced a lump of clay. "On the way home from kindergarten," she explained, "I stopped to watch some men digging a well. There was a lot of clay in the hole so I dug some up with my hands to bring to you. Will you please make me an animal?"

Runzi was intrigued. She had always been interested in arts and crafts, and taking the clay in her hands she began to mould a panda. The figure turned out successfully and other children began begging Runzi to make animals for them. Her success sustained her and a long suppressed artistic urge was aroused, bringing new life and hope. She acquired more of the clay and she was soon out of bed and working on her new hobby. Her husband's tender, loving care, her daughter's devotion, and her new found hobby were more potent medicines than any the doctor's could prescribe. When I went to visit Runzi in her studio in Beijing in 1991, she said to me,

"My clay figures gave me back my life. Now I give them life."

Intrigued by her new hobby, she began to study the faces of her daughter and her friends, and her figures soon developed character and a sense of reality. She branched out into figures representing heroes and heroines of both Chinese and foreign stories, one of the most outstanding being that of Jane Eyre whose childhood spoke to her of her own suffering.

Expanding her horizons, Runzi began to create figures taken from dance, theatre and folk opera. Unable to attend many public functions because they exhausted her energy, she studied art magazines, television and books on anatomy to help her create her imaginative figures.

As she progressed she began to investigate the various clays to find those more suitable for her sculptures. She developed such skill that her figures became known and students came to ask her to teach them. Her basic instructions were: first, you must love clay, and secondly you must get to know which is the right kind of clay for the work you want to do. When the President of Chinghau University saw her figures he was so impressed with her expertise that he asked if she would teach him.

As her work became known there were requests that she sell her creations, but she wouldn't do so.

"They are my children," she explained. "I cannot part with them"

Eventually a foreign delegation arrived in Beijing to acquire clay figures for an exhibition. The emphasis was on ancient sculpture, but one day a member of the delegation was exploring possibilities in a museum when he saw a long line-up of people. Intrigued by the interest they were showing, he investigated and discovered they were all eagerly seeking to view Runzi's clay figurines. He was so impressed with what he saw that he asked if he might go to Runzi's studio and see more of her work.

After the visit he returned to the hotel and suggested to the leader of the delegation that Zhang Runzi's figures were worthy of being included in their exhibition. The leader was unimpressed'

"Her work is too modern and she is not well enough known," he said

"Just come to her house for half an hour," urged his fellow member. "Come and see for yourself."

Reluctantly the leader agreed. At the end of half an hour the member waited for his leader to leave, but another half hour passed, and still another half hour before the delegation members left. Zhang Runzi's figures were included in the exhibition.

Zhang Runzi's small, mostly figurine sculptures, demonstrate a broad range of approaches to form and line. Quaint, colloquial figures that illustrate native stories and legends, such as the delightful group "The Girl and the Two Foxes" along with carefully moulded historical portraits from Chinese figures to foreign fictional characters offer a very varied collection of characters.

In much of her work the human body is pulled and given graceful but distorted curves and arcs that emphasize the willowy quality of Chinese femininity. Other figures, particularly pairs, are further abstracted, parts of the body having an exaggerated emphasis, massive bowed legs, broad plump hips and buttocks, or just the basic styalized human form linked into a rhythmic chain of human figures.

Movement characterizes her work. Dancers appear ready to step out to the rhythm of the dance, facial expressions and postures speak as clearly as words. Imagination has emancipated her from some of the traditional folk sculpture forms and offers variations in themes. She tries to convey beauty as she shapes the figures of antiquity, which has brought new life to ancient Chinese folk clay sculpture.

On her more representational figures she uses glazes to give colour and texture to garments. Graceful Tang dancers, musicians and their delicate instruments, ethnic minorities in their colourful garb, quaint cats, donkeys and camels, all add a delicate and fragile touch that is truly a part of herself.

More abstract forms tend to muted or colourless glazes. Prehistoric figures with their bows and arrows, shadowy figures from the past, including some from western lore, and even her exploration of mask-like reliefs, add a striking contrast.

Her figures have a flowing, romantic quality that pays tribute to her ability to overcome the hardships of the past and to express her gratitude for loving care that has mastered the effects of poverty and illness. To her it is a meaningful expression of new life and vitality. The wholeness of her characters suggest a successful healing process. The therapy of art linked to loving family relationships has restored this delightful artist to her country and her far-away friends.

Clay sculptures of the blind girl and foxes.

Springtime girl.

Deer and sheep.

Chapter 18

Practical Christian Dreamer
Liu Nian Fen

Liu Nian Fen on her visit to Canada at the United Church Camp, Shawnigan Lake

It was February 5, 1920. Nian Chu saw her grandfather coming through the gateway into their family compound. Running up to him, she exclaimed, "Grandfather, I have a new baby sister."

"Sister number four, eh?" said grandfather. "Now you have three sisters and two brothers."

"And I'm going to look after her," said Nian Chu, "because now I'm eight I can take care of her."

Grandfather looked at his eldest granddaughter and smiled at her youthful enthusiasm and ardent concern.

"Have you a name for little sister?" he asked as they walked to the spacious house of his eldest son.

"Her name is Nian-fen" (flower) said older sister proudly.

Two younger sisters and two brothers joined them as they entered the house. Grandmother was there, bustling about, helping the servant prepare the evening meal for the family. Almost immediately father appeared and was greeted with the news of the newest arrival. Then all sat down to eat after father had asked a blessing on the meal and on the newest member of the family.

"Did they launch the new boat today?" asked the boys

"Yes," said grandfather. "Your father and I both saw it safely into the river."

The brothers never ceased to be interested in the ships that came out of the docks where their grandfather and father worked. Ichang was a busy city on the banks of the mighty Yangtze River, and father was an accountant and grandfather a builder in one of the big shipbuilding yards.

Grandfather had come from the farm to Ichang to make a new life for himself. He had bought extensive property from time to time and with careful investment had built for himself and his sons, good two-storey homes for their growing families.

Little Nian-fen's lusty voice could be heard from the nearby bedroom demanding her dinner too. Nian Chu ran into her mother's room to look again at baby sister.

As the days passed, big sister took on responsibility for the younger children. Even at eight years of age she displayed a knack for leadership. But it was little sister, Nian-fen, whom she dearly loved. But more and more responsibility fell on her shoulders as three more sisters and another brother were added to the family.

It was a happy family. Father was a dedicated elder in the Christian church, and he and his wife brought up their ten children with a sense of values and a deep religious conviction that was nurtured by the Anglican church in their community. Nian Chu learned to sing and play the organ, leading all the children in family sing-songs and helping with family worship and with the children's studies.

Father Liu looked at his family and longed for one of them to take up the work of the church as a lifelong vocation. As the children, dressed in their best Sunday jackets, trooped off to church with their parents, father was stirred by little Nian-fen's spirit. Alert and always busy, she pulled at his heartstrings. This middle one of the seven daughters seemed to him to be the answer to his prayers. He often talked to her of his desire for one of his children to be dedicated to the service of the church and she responded to his challenge. At seven years of age Nian-fen was blessed by her father and dedicated by him to be especially nurtured in the Christian faith.

Father Liu saw to it that all his family received an education. Nian-fen attended the primary and junior high school in Ichang run by the Anglican missionaries, but when it came time for her to attend senior high school there was nothing available for her in Ichang. But older sister Nian Chu was by this time a college graduate and she immediately began teaching and supported three of her sisters through their high school and college education in the not too distant city of Wuhan.

By the time Nian-fen graduated from Wuhan University, the war with Japan was raging and she had to move to Sichuan province in the southeast of China. She worked with the YM and YW student centre in Leshan and there met two very dear friends, Katharine Hockin and her mother, missionaries with the United Church of Canada, who were a powerful influence in her life.

Throughout the war Nian-fen worked with students until fighting ceased in Wuhan. Returning to this badly disorganized and bombed city she set to work to find a place for a student centre. A rich business man's summer home attracted her attention and she was able to reach an agreement with him to use the property and some of the buildings for a college students' centre. Part of the agreement included a promise by Nian-fen to set up two primary schools for children in the surrounding countryside. The farmers found a small place, the children brought their own tables and chairs, and the YM and YW paid student teachers to staff the schools. One of Nian-fen's dreams had come true.

Through 1945 to 1947 Liu Nian-fen nurtured the students of Wuhan University with classes in Bible study, worship and general studies, her job as student secretary paid by the National Chinese YM

In 1947 a brother-in-law, by that time Vice-Principal of Wuhan University, helped Nian-fen to get a one year scholarship to Winter Park College in California. Through Katharine and Mrs. Hockin and other friends she was able the following year to secure a scholarship to Union Theological College in New York and received her MA in Religious Education in 1950.

Meanwhile the Revolution of 1949 had begun to change the face of China. Liu Nian-fen returned to her homeland, dedicated to serving her people and her church. She was appointed General Secretary of the YWCA for her province of Hubei, but there were no buildings and the city was devastated. But misfortune never deterred Nian-fen. Through hard work and the assistance of some Swedish missionaries the Y headquarters were built. No sooner had she accomplished this than in 1950 she went to Shanghai for a few months to work in the YM-YW national office, but soon returned to Wuhan as General Secretary.

Her first effort in Wuhan was to start a kindergarten, but the project that attracted her most was a ministry to the many women with comfortable incomes and time on their hands who had no schooling. She set up a school for these women from 9 to 11 a.m. and 2 to 4 p.m. so that they had time for their home duties as well as study. Over a number of years these women were able to graduate from senior high school with additional expertise in sewing, first aid and other home skills. For them it was then only a step to remunerative positions in the new burgeoning economy.

It was at this time that romance entered Nain-fen's life. Dr. Gao, a leading specialist in pediatrics who had studied in Japan for ten years, lost his wife and was left with four children. His admiration for the work of Liu Nian-fen culminated in a proposal and in 1958 they were married. Nian-fen, now 38 years of age, made it very clear that she could not give up her tremendously busy schedule, but Dr. Gao was a very understanding man and he assumed a large portion of the home responsibility. At 40 Nian-fen had her first and only child, and the blended family grew up happily together.

In 1966 the dark days of the Cultural Revolution loomed. All religious institutions were closed, all assets frozen. The YM, the YW, and the churches could no longer operate. However, the five different religious institutions, Protestant, Catholic, Buddhist, Moslem and Taoist, organized a committee of five and urged the government to release their funds so that they could co-operatively carry out a useful program. They undertook:

1. To translate documents, because of their knowledge of various languages
2. To carry on sewing classes to make clothes for the people
3. To make funeral sprays.

Funds from these enterprises were to be carefully monitored by accountants and were to be used for community services. The government finally released the funds and the committee carried on the work for the ten years duration of the Cultural Revolution. By 1978, property was returned to the religious organizations and since then the co-operative spirit has been maintained and the five religious groups work in harmony in the community.

Liu Nian-fen never lost her dream. Reaching out to the community was for her the bridge between the church and society. She formed young people's groups where students learned English, German, French or improved their knowledge of Chinese, and they had the opportunity to study music and piano. Not all the students who came to these classes were Christians but many became active church members and shared in church concerts and activities. Service to the community also dominated her programs and young people were often sent to the aid of the elderly or young children.

But Nian-fen's dearest dream was the establishment of a theological seminary for the training of church leaders. With no money, no staff and no students she began to plan and work. Amazingly within months her dream became a reality when in 1985 the Central South China Theological Seminary was opened in Wuchang, a suburb of Wuhan. Unfortunately her husband died in 1978 and shortly afterwards she lost her mother. "It was just my strong faith in God's grace that saw me through," she said, "and therefore I must thank God by working for Him with all my heart and strength." She supported her son through college after which he taught physical education and lectured part time at the seminary

With the opening of the theological seminary, Liu Nian-fen was made President, a position she has continued to hold. At the same time at 72 years of age she was a Member of the Standing Committee of the China Christian Council, Chair of Hubei Christian Council, was General Secretary of the Wuhan YWCA, and was elected a Member of the Standing Committee of Hubei People's Congress (provincial legislature).

But as if this wasn't enough, she insists there are four things she still plans to do:

1. Improve the seminary, develop a larger faculty
2. Continue to reach out to the local churches to help them solve their problems
3. Help them get back expropriated property and build local churches. There are 380 churches and meeting places under the care of the seminary, many of which she visits, preaching, teaching and counselling.
4. Build a new building for the Seminary so that there is accommodation for 120 student.
5. Develop better programs to help the elderly.

Describing the type of work that the Seminary does for the outlying churches, she described to me one of her experiences.

"At Christmas, 1989, the students and faculty went to Dayei. The church seats 500. On Christmas Eve our choir sang, the students and faculty told the Christmas story and conducted a beautiful worship service. No sooner was the service over than people who were lined up outside waiting for the first group to come out, filed into the church and the service was repeated. The following morning the church was packed three times over. We had 2,500 people on that one visit. And they didn't come for the service and then go home. Cooks kept food going. The whole celebration cost 2,000 yuan ($475) but the money was all contributed by the people as well as food, wood for the fires, and other essentials."

To conclude the story she added, "I don't want any special treatment. We all slept on beds of hay, the women in one large room, and the men in another. We don't ask for any privileges on these visits."

Barely five feet tall, Liu Nian-fen gives thanks for her strong constitution and then proceeds to make her dreams a reality. In 1991 she visited Canada and I took her to a church camp. There she swam with the campers and then talked to them around the campfire. It was a memorable experience. She exudes a warm and sparkling spirit and talks in terms of a world-wide community of faith that transcends all national barriers

She's the stuff of which modern women in China are made.

from left: Chaplain Ge Buo Juan, Pastor Wang Dianchang, author, President Liu Nian Fen, Wang Chuzie, gov't rep from Dept. of Religion, the 1991 delegation to Canada

Chapter 19

From Camel Tender's Daughter to Fashion Clothes Executive
Qian Xiuzhen

Qian Xiuzhen in her apartment

I was to interview Qian Xiuzhen, Manager of the prestigious Xin Xin Fashion Clothes Store, strangely located in a maze of ten-foot wide back streets in the capital of China, Beijing.

When the taxi that my interpreter and I had hired turned off the broad thoroughfare, the first obstacle apart from people and bicycles, was a truck parked in front of a convenience store. It was totally impossible to pass so for 15 minutes we sat behind the vehicle while the driver loaded 24 cases of empty pop bottles on to his truck. When it finally took off we made a sharp right-hand turn on to a road momentarily clear. But suddenly a large van confronted us and one of us had to give way. Our driver, backing cautiously through the crowd, eased around a corner to let the van pass, a masterful manoeuvre that was repeated several times while bicycles, hand carts, tricycles and humans slipped around us.

Within sight of our destination we approached cautiously as it seemed that half the population of Beijing had chosen this Saturday to renew their wardrobes. The taxi, proceeding at a snail's pace, had to negotiate a turn, but at a 45° angle encountered a metal hand cart jammed against a brick wall. A crowd five deep completely surrounded our car, with masses of shoppers converging on all sides. I envisioned being trapped until the store closed.

In spite of the scraping of the iron cart on the taxi door, the driver moved gingerly forward an inch at a time. After 20 minutes we finally negotiated the turn and found the Deputy Manager of the store patiently waiting for us on the front steps. It had taken nearly an hour to travel six short blocks!

We were immediately led up four flights of concrete steps to the Manager's sitting room where we were received by Madame Qian Xiuzhen, a handsome and graceful woman of 53. Dressed fashionably in a short skirt, lace blouse, nylons and pumps, she sat in a comfortable upholstered chair and invited us to enjoy the customary welcoming cup of tea. Her black, lightly curled hair fell softly around her face, a self-possessed woman with a twinkle in her eye and a gracious manner. Willingly she talked to us and told us her story.

Born in 1938 of a very poor Wei minority family in the countryside on the outskirts of Beijing, Qian Xiuzhen had no opportunity for an early education. She never attended school until she was twelve years of age.

"Why not?" she asked and then answered her own question. "Because it was considered a waste of time to educate a girl. Besides, my father tended camels and loaded them with coal for transporting to distant places. We were very poor. My mother died when I was five years old, and my little brother just three. My father remarried and two stepsisters were added to the family. I had to help with the house work and care for the younger children."

"But you did say you went to school when you were twelve," I said

"Yes, when Liberation came in 1949 I was able to go to night school. I couldn't go in the daytime because I was needed at home, but I did complete primary school in three years. Then because I am of Wei nationality I was allowed to attend the Minority Nationalities School in Beijing. After one year there I began at the age of 16 to work in a department store. I went back to night school and finally completed middle school."

Being a very attractive girl Xiuzhen was admired by many of the young men in the nationalities school and the night school, but young people at that time did not mix freely. With a smile and a twinkle in her eye, however, she admitted that Xue Shu Hua, a classmate four years her senior, had fallen in love with her, although they had hardly spoken to each other.

In 1955 Xiuzhen was assigned to a department store where she became a telephone operator, then an elevator operator, and eventually a sales girl. One day she and Shu Hua met in the store where it turned out that they were both working.

"Oh, you were my classmate," said Shu Hua by way of introduction. As both were Wei nationality they ate in the special restaurant for Moslems and became better acquainted over meals.

In 1956 China established an army service group of volunteers chosen from the best young men in the land. Shu Hua, a member of the Communist Youth League, and top quality worker, volunteered and was readily accepted for three years service. When interviewed he was asked if he had any problems or concerns.

"Yes," he replied. "I want to marry Qian Xiuzhen."

The secretary of the Youth League told Xiuzhen of the "proposal" and advised her that Shu Hua was a very good and desirable man. Although she was young and very pretty and popular, she agreed that the match was a good one and that she really cared for him.

When his three year army stint was over, the couple were married in 1961. Two boys were born to Qian and Xue in 1962 and 1968. Meanwhile Xiuzhen had joined and worked hard in the Communist Youth League so that in 1965 she was made a cadre, an organizer and supervisor of staff.

But life was not to be a bed of roses. With the onslaught of the Cultural Revolution in 1966 many people suffered. Qian Xiuzhen was torn from her family in 1971 and sent to work on a farm, fortunately not far from Beijing, where she planted rice and tended the orchard. Her husband was not sent away so was able to care for the two little boys.

After one year Xiuzhen was allowed to return to her work and she continued at the store, at the same time developing her favourite hobby of reading. Finally in 1974 the Xin Xin Fashion Store was opened and she was transferred and made Deputy Secretary of the Communist Party for workers, designed to keep them informed on government policy and development in their fields.

By 1979 her organizing ability and sales management had become apparent and she was made Manager of the fast growing Xin Xin Fashion Clothing Store. As the store grew in size and prestige, Xiuzhen, from 1988-90, was given specialized management training courses in the afternoon while still being responsible for her regular work.

When I interviewed her in 1991, seven hundred employees worked under her direction. She herself chose many of the clothes for which the store became famous. She also did some designing and drew up contracts with a subsidiary factory for making uniforms for various institutions. The organization had also grown from being strictly retail to include a factory and eventually a hotel had been added to the complex.

Under the guidance of competent parents, the couple's two boys have attended university and one has become an aeronautical engineer, the other a computer specialist working with his father who is Manager of the Travel Department of the Friendship Store.

From an illiterate camel tender's daughter to mother of two highly successful boys and Manager of a Fashion Clothing-Hotel Complex in 40 years in a city of 12 million people is no small achievement. It is no wonder Qian Xiuzhen was featured in a widely read publication of outstanding women entrepreneurs in modern China.

inside the fashion store

Chapter 20

Matriarchal Societies
Where Women Rule

The head of a matrilineal family. The bunch of keys on her belt is a symbol of power.⁶

Chinese history records periods of matriarchal rule. In the ancient city of Xian there is a group statue of women who reportedly governed the area probably during what is known as the Yangchao Culture some 6,000 to 7,000 years ago. At this time people had began to live in groups as members of a clan. They had learned to make stone and bone instruments, had developed skills in pottery, and agriculture and animal husbandry were beginning to have a place in their society. With these developments came also skill in spinning and weaving and the knowledge of house building, which led to a more sedentary life. In Xian the Bampo Village site shows a typical community with a reconstructed house built on the actual site of an ancient settlement. It is here that the statue of women indicates the presence of a matriarchal society.

Today in a remote valley in Yunnan province there still exists a branch of the Naxi minority who have lived until quite recently, and still do to a certain extent, live according to the primitive pairing system that is matrilineal in structure.

I first heard about this strange society from General Wu when we were travelling with him to the celebrations for Dr. Bethune in 1989. He claimed he had visited the tribe but I thought he was "pulling my leg" when he described the customs. However, I later met a Canadian radio producer who had worked with Radio Beijing and had subsequently travelled through China visiting about forty of the fifty-six nationalities in the country. She also had visited in this remote area and confirmed General Wu's stories. Finally in a book on Chinese Minorities and a magazine article on "The Naxi People of Lugu Lake" in China Pictorial, I was reassured that the strange tales of these people were true.

The tribe known as the Mosuo live on the shores of Lugu Lake, between Yunnan and Sichuan provinces, and their ancient customs and language have been passed down from the dim past. At the north end of the lake is Lion Hill, regarded as a goddess called Gammu who controls the prosperity of the people, their livelihood, and their personal lives. She is pictured riding a magnificent white horse with the clouds for a wreath around her head. The verdant growth on the hillside is her clothing and her feet are clad in the coral and agate at her base. Her beauty enraptures the mountain gods around her who enjoy the liberty of unrestricted love relationships with her.

In the latter part of June a day is set aside to celebrate her rendezvous with the gods, and everyone puts on his or her festive clothes and joins the worshippers at the hill. Many young men and women find this an occasion to search for lovers and enjoy their own tryst, pitching a tent or finding a mountain retreat.

When boys and girls become of age at 13 they take part in a "trouser" and "skirt" ceremony according to their sex, and from then on intercourse between them in acceptable. They are free to meet one another at dances and fairs, on the street or in the fields. They can choose their partners freely except for members of the same maternal family.

Datiao, a popular dance of the Mosuos, offers an opportunity for young men and women to meet each other. In the early evening they array themselves in their most attractive clothes and gather to light a bonfire. When the piper arrives and begins to play, some of the young men begin to dance. The young women single out the men who capture their fancy, take their hands and begin to dance with them. As the fire blazes higher and higher more and more dancers arrive. Singing lustily, the crowd of hundreds begins to whirl in a large circle or follow a leader in a convoluted column, with rhythmic stamping of feet and shouts that reverberate through the hills. By the end of the evening couples have chosen their partners and leave for their respective retreats.

In every day life a young man may go to the house of the girl he favours, taking a gift. If the gift is acceptable to the women of the house, he may stay the night. The couple are then considered to be "azhu" which means friend or lover, but each continues to live at home. Each morning young men can be seen returning from their azhus' to their mothers' homes where they still reside. In the daytime they work their mother's land and have no responsibility whatsoever to their azhu or her family.

Cohabitation may be temporary or permanent, lasting only for a night or two, but might stretch to a few months or occasionally to a year. Most men and women have at least six or seven azhus during their lifetime. Sometimes an exchange of scarves or rings takes place, or the young man may simply appropriate something that belongs to the girl of his choice, but if she smiles it is an indication of her agreement to an Azhu partnership.

This partnership does not entail any financial responsibilities. Either party to the arrangement is free to break the relationship at any time. The door may be closed to the young man, or he may cease to visit. If a child is born, he or she is brought up by the women of the family who form the economic basis of the society. The family line is traced through the mothers, the child takes the mother's name, and all property is passed down through the female line. The male offspring lives in his mother's home and these adult males are known as uncles. They share in the care of the children and assist in tasks in the mother's home. The women are the organizers, administer the affairs of society, and are supreme in decision making.

There is no word for "father" and many children have no idea who their "father" is. A family consists of grandmother and the two or three generations of women in the household, but the head woman does not claim special privileges. Everything belongs to all, except for a few items of clothing or small personal belongings.

The older women and children sleep in the main hall around the hearth, and it is in this room that the "family" meets for meals, discussions, entertainment of guests, and the offering of sacrifices to the gods and ancestors. The women sit on the right of the hearth in the place of greater honour, while the men sit on the left. On one side of the hall there is a room in which the old men of the family live, but every woman has a room of her own where she may receive her Azhu lover or lovers. The young men, however, have no rooms of their own. When they are not visiting their Azhu they stay in the old men's room in their mother's house.

Cut off from outside influences by the isolated nature of their valley, the Naxi people have tended to retain their ancient customs and social structure. However, with modernization, economic reform and closer communications, the azhu system tends to give way. In 1956 a survey showed that 93% of the families were matrilineal or a mixture of matrilineal and patrilineal, and it was obvious from General Wu's and the CBC visitor's observations in the 1980's that the matrilineal system was still in operation.

The constitution of China guarantees that every nationality may keep its habits and customs, but many Naxi people are beginning to side with the government in their desire to implement the marriage laws, moving step by step to a monogamous society. It is to be hoped that Naxi women will not lose their powerful position in the new society that evolves.

Chapter 21

Twelve Women of National Minorities Introduce Themselves

Minority women studying at the Institute of Magerial Cadres of Wemen in Beijing.
Author right centre first row, Guide interpreter left first row

China has 56 nationalities included in her population. Of these the Han represent the major portion, being 93% of the total. The other 55 nationalities are scattered, largely in the north and southeast, with 26 of them living in the province of Yunnan. The smallest groups like the Oroquen and Hezhen number only 2,000 to 3,000, partly because their population was gradually assimilated by other larger nationalities, and partly because they were so exploited and oppressed that poverty and disease nearly wiped them out. By 1945 the Hezhen numbered only 300 but have since regained their numbers but remain the smallest ethnic group.

At one time largely ignored and looked down on, the minority nationalities are now being encouraged to develop their cultures and at the same time become active participants in the new China. For the most part they are not restricted in the number of children they may have although the larger minorities are advised to have not more than two children.

Schools in the minority areas may conduct their first grades in their national language but Mandarin is required in the upper grades. Special universities and training schools are built for national minorities to encourage them to prepare for community service and government jobs.

In November of 1991 I was invited to interview twelve women of different nationalities at the Institute of Managerial Cadres of Women where they were pursuing studies to improve their skills for work in the communities. Very briefly they told me their stories.

Tung

Wu De Fang was a 23 year old woman of the Tung nationality from Guizhou province where a large proportion of the 1.3 million people of her nationality reside. She had been a primary school teacher for three years but left this career to work at the county level for the All China Women's Federation. Feeling the need for more training, she enrolled in the Institute to improve her skills.

Women of the Tung nationality have always been held in high respect, a rare attitude in old China. Women could succeed to family wealth, whereas sons could not, and when a woman married she could bring land to the marriage. Women were considered the creators and controllers of wealth. They were also free to have sexual relationships with men at the woman's home, and children took the mother's name at birth. Widows were allowed to remarry, an uncommon right in other nationalities prior to Liberation in 1949.

Women played an important role in the political struggle, often sending information on bandits and illegal procedures to the government.

Many women are now going to college and serving as high-ranking officials. The leader of the Guizhou Provincial Women's Federation and many of the county heads are women of the Tung nationality.

Lisu

From an area in Yunnan province in the extreme southwest came Mei Xui Fang, 25 years of age, of the Lisu nationality. She had been a kindergarten teacher for five years and had come to the Institute to study the management of children in their pre-school and kindergarten years.

The Lisu people have a population of about half a million and have their own distinctive language. Their ancestors settled around the rivers of the southeast before the 8th century and divided into three tribes distinguished by the colours of their dress: the White Lisu, the Black Lisu and the Variegated Lisu.

Because the climate is warm in the valleys the Lisu build their houses of bamboo on stilts and their animals are housed under the floor. Agriculture is their main occupation with tangerine oranges as a major crop. Hot springs afford excellent gathering places for bathing and musical jamborees

Xui Fang assured us that music and dancing are very much a part of their culture. Their Fairs, New Year celebrations and weddings are occasions of great festivities that last for days. Wine is abundant and everyone participates in the merriment to the music of flutes and stringed instruments. Not only do the young people sing to each other, but the parents of the bride and groom make up verses about their children and sing them antiphonally.

It is no surprise that the Lisu are known as "The Merry Nationality." One of their favourite sayings is "Only the dead should be deprived of a mirthful life."

Manchu

The Manchu Nationality traces its roots to the Manchu dynasty, the last imperial rulers of China. Twenty-eight year old Jin Yen, from the province of Sichuan, claims a grandfather who belonged to the imperial family that was overthrown by the 1911 revolution. The four million Manchu people are scattered in many parts of China, largely in the northern provinces where most engage in agriculture.

However, Jin Fen's family moved to the southwest. Her parents settled in the province of Sichuan when Jen Fen was three years of age. She grew up in new China with a special concern for students from minority nationalities of which there are many in her province.

For two years she had been a kindergarten teacher but she encountered many problems and, deciding she needed further training, she registered at the Institute. Before she became a teacher she had worked in a factory and played on the factory basketball team. But her concern and love for children of the minorities led her into teaching and eventually into further study so that she could use the best methods to develop the potential of her students.

Mongolian

From the northern grassland of inner Mongolia came 25 year old Zao Jin Yu. Specializing in chemistry in high school she was assigned upon graduation to a rubber factory. However, she felt that her knowledge and training were not adequate to meet the requirements of her work, so she enrolled in the Institute and is training in the secretarial field.

Inner Mongolia is a vast landscape three or four thousand feet above sea level, a land of mountains, deserts and rolling plains. The grassland is one of the major husbandry areas of China. Huge flocks of sheep and goats roam the open spaces, camels are bred for their usefulness in the desert areas, and the Mongolian pony is famous for its fleetness and strength. With economic development large factories have been established to tap the resources of the area, turning the wool into cloth and garments, producing lumber from the forests, and minerals from the extensive mines and alkaline lakes.

All this development has led to huge increases in the number of industrial workers, primary and secondary schools, technical institutes and research projects in which women are playing a part. Jin Yu, therefore, came to the Institute to expand her understanding of the new era in Mongolian life that has seen a phenomenal rise in the people's living standards and a demand for higher education to cope with the rapidly changing society.

But it isn't all work and no play in Mongolia. "My people," said Jin Yu, "are very fond of singing and dancing and at our annual Nadam Fair we gather from all over Inner Mongolia for horse racing, archery, wrestling, entertainment and many modern sports."

I could personally attest to the outstanding quality of their dancing and singing as I have been privileged to see several performances by Mongolian song and dance troupes.

Jin Yu also spoke with pride of outstanding women in Mongolian history who she felt had contributed to important events in the past.

Zhuang

The southeastern province of Guangxi is the home of Feng Hui Jun, a member of the largest minority in China, the Zhuang, with a population of more than 14 million who are scattered through four provinces. Many Zhuang hold important government positions.

Hui Jun told us with pride that as a young woman she had been an ardent basketball player and had been a member of the provincial team. Some ten years older than most of the women we interviewed, she told us that she was married to a soldier and had a seven year old child. She had spent several years as a factory worker but because of her interest in women's work she had applied to and been accepted by the Women's Federation for work with the women of her province. She was an enthusiastic promoter of her province where many of her nationality live. She explained that the Zuang people are largely involved in agriculture, growing rice, corn, potatoes, sugar cane, lichee and dragon's eye fruit, and exporting spices.

However, Hui Jun felt that her people were most famous for their beautiful embroidery and their folk songs. Both of these arts are used in their courting. When a young couple are interested in one another they compose songs that they sing back and forth. If the young man presents his partner with a cloth handkerchief she may embroider a floral design or throw an embroidered ball to the young man signifying her affection. The compact is then sealed.

Feng Hui Jun recalled that the Long March had crossed her province and her people had given help to Mao Tse-tung and received benefits from that contact. Her story was warm-hearted and helpful, characteristic of the people she represented, and her parting remark was an invitation to all present to attend the national sports meet soon to be held in her province.

Yi

Representing the Yi nationality was 27 year old Hua Xin Tin from Guizhou province who opened her interview by singing a delightful provincial folk song which drew applause from all present. She then went on to say that she had worked for the Women's Federation in her town and then in 1984 for the general affairs department in charge of children's work. Sensing her lack of enough training and knowledge, she looked for a centre where she could develop her skills and she chose the Institute because of its national standing. As her work entailed writing reports and articles, she chose to study the secretarial course.

Xin Tin pointed out that marriage had previously been arranged by parents, but now young people were deciding for themselves who their partners would be. The emancipation of women was, therefore, one of her interests and she wanted to study in this field. The wedding ceremony, she explained, was a very festive affair with music and dancing and much horn blowing.

The Yi people are very scattered in many parts of China with only 20,000 of the five and a half million Yi in China actually living in her province. "We are a very hospitable people," she assured us, "and visitors are greeted with a cup of corn or rice wine and walnuts. Please come and visit us."

Miao

The five million Miao people, like the Yi, are scattered through many provinces and even into the northern part of Thailand that borders south China. Yu Hong, 23 years of age, is an accountant in a garment factory in Guizhou province, or as she expressed it, "I'm from the watermelon country." But as she said, rice is another major crop. According to legend one of their early chieftains, tired of hunting, persuaded his people to fill in the marshlands and create rice paddies. We have a saying, she related, that "if there is no music in the home, the rice will not grow."

Music is an essential part of Miao culture. Hosts sing to their guests who reply in song. Disputes and quarrels are often solved through songs, and the sound of a familiar tune played on a bamboo reed will bring a young girl out to meet her lover. Love songs and embroidered balls play a part in Miao courting customs. Wedding ceremonies and festivals are replete with horns, pipes, other musical instruments, and much dancing Their colourful costumes, massive silver jewellery and extraordinary hair dos vie with their exquisite embroidery to make them one of the most interesting minorities in China.

I personally have a magnificent embroidered skirt that the gentleman who sold it to me at a market high in the hills, told me it took his mother a full year to embroider the skirt alone. I can believe it for the finely pleated skirt measures yards around and is covered with cross stitch, appliquéd designs and decorated ribbon strips that makes it an outstanding piece of handwork. The Miao are known as the outstanding embroiderers of China.

The Maio people have a history of 2,600 years. They are a progressive people who, Yu Hong explained, have now opened up their areas to the outside world. They have participated in reform and as a result living standards have risen enormously so that many families now have washing machines, television and other amenities

Bulong

Zhao Jia Zhen, a 34 year old mother of a ten-year old son, had been active in Women's Federation work in Yunnan province since 1978. Her sphere of interest was in family planning, and in 1984 she undertook the study of law with a view to safeguarding the rights of women and children of the 60,000 members of the Bulong nationality.

Happily married to a man who is a technician in a rubber factory, Zhao undertook the arduous trip of seven days and nights to reach Beijing because she felt that her knowledge was not sufficient to meet the requirements of her work. She told how she regretfully left her happy family for a time in order to gain the knowledge required to carry on her work successfully.

She recalled the days when her people were oppressed by landlords but "now," she said, "we are the masters, we are united in our desire to establish a just society".

With a smile she invited me to visit her home in the province of Yunnan where her Bulong people live.

Wa

Li Hung Fang, 24 years of age, was a little reticent about speaking of her WA minority in Yunnan province, who number about 300,000. It is a rugged area near the Burmese border and was once described as "a barren and savage land", poor and backward, where bandits roamed and blood feuds erupted in the villages. It was a centre of the opium trade and was one of the last places to eliminate slavery.

The area is, however, rich in mineral resources, valuable trees and medicinal herbs, and the fertile soil makes cultivation easy. The difficulty is that there is hardly a single piece of level land as big as a playing field. Until recently the Wa people were destitute and oppressed but the problem of insufficient food has now been solved and the people are working hard to develop cash crops such as tea and mangos. Forestry is also now coming into its own as the barren hills have been planted with fir and pine.

It is not to be wondered that Hung Fang upon graduation from high school threw in her lot with the Women's Federation for whom she worked for five years. She specialized in solving family disputes and safeguarding the legitimate rights of women and children and of her minority people. She soon realized the inadequacy of her knowledge and training, and came to the Institute to further prepare herself for the great task that lay before her.

Hui

Representing the Hui nationality in Ningzia province was 34 year old Li Shu Yin. The seven million Hui people are Moslem, scattered through a number of provinces in the north-west where the Arabic and Persian influence predominated during the Song and Tang dynasties (618-1279 AD). Following this period, Mongolians returning from expeditions to the Middle East strengthened the Muslim faith.

Ningxia is known as an autonomous state, indicating that the Hui people have predominant control of their area in co-operation with the national government. Muslim rites and customs predominate. "Wedding ceremonies," Shu Yin explained, "are not legitimate unless conducted according to Muslim ritual. We also observe the month long feast of

Ramadam."

"We are also very proud of our water conservancy and irrigation programme, our university and our academy of sciences. The standard of living in our area has risen unbelievably."

After graduating from high school Li Shu Yin joined the staff of the Women's Federation, working first as an accountant and then began handling letters and complaints and sometimes court cases related to women and children. In the old society Hui women were the most inhumanly treated of all women in China's minority groups. Women are still being discriminated against but conditions are steadily improving. More and more Hui women are becoming leaders in their townships and counties and are proving successful in the arts and sports, formerly forbidden to them. Incidentally Su Yin mentioned that the production of rose cosmetic oil for export has opened up numerous jobs for women.

Minority people are allowed to have two children and Shu Yia, who was married in 1980, has two daughters. She came to the Institute to gain a more adequate background for assisting women in her province.

Dai

In the south-western part of Yunnan province there are many people of the Dai nationality who belong to the same culture as the people of Thailand. The climate is tropical and houses are very open and spacious and often on stilts.

"My people are Buddhist," said twenty-four year old Zhou Li Hing, "and have many beautiful temples and pagodas. We like to live near water, as water is considered 'lucky' ". The spring water-splashing ceremony is well known both inside and outside of China and is a time of much merry-making and courting. Like many minorities, love songs are an important part of courting and wedding ceremonies are very festive occasions.

Li Hing pointed out that in 1984 legislation in China enhanced the position of minorities and assured them that 85% of the cadres (organizers and supervisors) must be of the nationality they serve. Since 1984 she had been involved in women's work which she claimed at times is very complicated since it also involved working with men. There were so many factors, she said, that influenced life in their society that she longed to study further. She had been married four years but had no children, as she was too involved in her studies. Because there is no strong legal system in China, particularly in relation to minority people, she felt the need to study law at the Institute so that she could return to serve her people better.

Bai

Yang Biao Ru, 28 years of age, hailed from Yunnan province where she had begun women's work in 1984 in the field of safeguarding the rights of women and children. Like several of the other women she realized that in order to solve problems and protect those rights it was necessary for her to have a knowledge of law. Consequently she came to the Institute and enrolled in the law department in preparation for her future work.

Like so many of the minority people, Biao Ru talked of the love of the people for dancing and singing and the use of songs for love making. Their annual Sanyuejie Fair dates back more than a thousand years, and caravans of other minority people come from far-away places bringing their goods for trading. It is a time for great festivity, dance jamborees, opera, games and exhibitions.

Biao Ru mentioned a film entitled "Five Golden Flowers" recently produced by the Bai nationality which, she said, was now being made available to people outside China through the Chinese Embassies.

Uigher people from the west of China intermarried with Arabian visitors travelling via the Silk Road

On Love Making and Law Making

As mentioned in many of the above stories, courting is often carried on by song. To illustrate, here is a courting song of the Dai nationality, translated by the New Zealander, Rewi Alley, who spent most of his adult life in China working with the people and learning their language and culture.

At the Feast

Lass:
Today when guests are many
do not steal glances at me
so often, letting others
know our secret, so that they
may come to tease me! For
how can I tell them of it;
where can I go to hide from them?
When I came, I thought
better not to recognize you!
But who would have known
when I caught your eyes, how
they magnetized me; for when
they met, my heart pounded,
my face covered with blushes.

Lad:
Girl, don't try to hide behind
the bodies of other folk, playing
at not knowing me never saying
even one word to me! and why
do you put up your hands to cover

your face, then through open fingers
look hard at me?

Lass:
My dear, do not drink
so much wine, for if you are drunk
then we cannot meet tonight:
Use your flute and play louder;
sing more of those love songs
that rise straight from your heart.

Lad:
Beloved, do not be for ever
staring at me, for if you
look at me like that, I can play
Nothing on my flute, and from my throat
song can no longer come, for it
will be as though a shell
has stuck right there.

Lass:
Dear when you sing, do not
put your fan in front of your face
for I would have the sound come
straight into my heart, and then
the handkerchief I gave you, do not
for ever be pulling it out
to wipe you lips, so that our secret
all around will know!

Lad:
On the festival day of throwing water
why did you chase me, throwing so much?
For you poured so much on me
that I was like a half drowned hen;
and if my heart had not kept me warm
I should have caught my death of cold. [7]

Because of the demand for legal protection for women and children the National Congress in 1992 passed overwhelmingly the law on the "Protection of Women's Rights and Interests of the People's Republic of China" which came into effect October 2, 1992. This document will be an important part of the law studies at the Institute, but as several leading women have pointed out, while the law greatly improves the quality of life for women, the State should exert more effort to increase the proportion of women participating in the political life of the country. Women still do not have a place in the upper echelons of national power.

The magazine *Women of China* features many articles on problems "Legal Challenges to Women", "The Psychological Emancipation of Women", "Women and Development" "Illiteracy Among Women," "Economic Independence, the Key to Improved Status and Role." The women at the Institute of Managerial Cadres of Women are well aware of these problems and it was interesting to meet these lively women who were studying to tackle the problems in their own communities.

Some of the national minority costumes.

Permissions

1. Chapter 6, Li Ching Chao. "Yellow bodies, light in colour and weight" *Complete Poems of Li Ch'ing Chao* (alternative spelling for Li Quing Zhao). Permission granted by New Directions Publishing Corporation, N.Y.

2. Chapter 6, Li Ching Chao. "Evening comes with the onslaught of wind and rain". *The Columbia Book of Chinese Poetry*. Permission granted by Columbia University Press N.Y.

3. Chapter 6, Li Ching Chao. "Deep in the silent room". Poem called *Remorse*, from *Complete Poems of Li Ch'ing Chao*. Permission granted by New Directions Publishing Corporation, N.Y.

4. Chapter 6, Li Ching Chao. "The River of Heaven turns across the sky", (Song of the South) from *Complete poems of Li Ch'ing Chao*. Permission granted by New Directions Publishing Corporation, N.Y.

5. Chapter 15, Bing Xin. "Stars, millions of stars" vs 1. Shoe String Press inc. Hamden, Conn.

6. Chapter 20, photo of Naxi woman courtesy of *China Today*, Beijing, China

7. Chapter 21, On Love Making and Law Making, *"At the Feast"* translated by Rewi Alley in *"Folk Poems from China's Minorities"*. Permission granted by New World Press, Beijing, China.

Bibliography

Alley, Rewi, *Folk Poems from China's Minorities*, translated by Rewi Alley New World Press, Beijing, 1984.

Bland J.D.P. & Backhouse E., *China Under the Empress Dowager,* William Heinemann, London, 1921.

Cambridge History of China, Vol. 1, Ch'in & Han Empires 221B.C. - 220 AD edited by Denis Twitchett & Michael Loewe
    Vol 3. Sui & T'ang, 589-906, Part 1 edited by Denis Twitchett
    Vol. 11, Late Ching, 1800-1911, John D. Fairbank & Kwang-Ching Liu. Cambridge University Press, Cambridge, 1979-1980.

Carl, Katharine, *With the Empress Dowager of China*, Century Co., New York 1907.

China's Minority Nationalities (1) published by China Reconstructs Press, Beijing 1985.

Cooney, Eleanor & Alieri, Daniel, *The Court of the Lion*, Avon Books, N. Y. 1990.

Departed But Not Forgotten - Women of China, published by Women of China, Beijing, distributed by China International Book Trading Corp., Beijing 1984.

Der Ling, Princess, first lady-in-waiting to the Empress Dowager, Two Years in the Forbidden City, copyright 1911 by Moffat, Yard & Co., New York, printed by Dodd Mead & Co., New York, 1924.

Ding Zuxin & Raffel, Burton, *Gems of Chinese Poetry*, Shoe String Press, Hamden, Connecticut, 1986.

Fitzgerald, C.P. *The Empress Wu*, Cresset Press, London, 1969

Guisso, R.W.L., *Wu Tse-T'ien and the Politics of Legitimation in T'ang China* Western Washington University, 1978.

Hahn, Emily, *Chiang Kai Shek* Doubleday & Co., Inc., Garden City, New York, 1955.

Hahn, Emily, *The Soong Sisters,* Garden City Publishing Co. Inc. Garden City, N.Y. 1941.

Haldane, Charlotte, *The Last Great Empress of China*, Constable, London, 1965.

Hibbert, Christopher, *The Emperors of China*, editor Charles L. Mee Jr. Tree Communications Inc. under supervision of Stonehenge Press Inc. R.R. Donnelly & Sons, U.S.A., 1981.

History, compiled by China Handbook Editorial Committee, translated by Duu. J. Li, Foreign Language Press, Beijing, 1982.

Hsu, Immanuel C. Y. *The Rise of Modern China*, Oxford University Press, London, 1975.

Hu Pin Ch'ing, Li Ch'ing Chao, editor Howard S. Levy, Twayne's World Authors Series, China, Twayne Publishers Inc., New York, 1966.

Llewellyn, George, *China's Courts & Concubines*, George Allen & Unwin, London 1985.

Li Nianfei, *Old Tales of China*, China Travel & Tourism Press, Beijing, 1985.

Ma Yin, chief compiler, *Questions and Answers about China's National Minorities,* New World Press, Beijing, 1985.

Po Chu-I, *Lament Everlasting*, translation and essays by Howard Levy, Tokyo, 1962.

Rexroth, Kenneth & Ling Chung, translators and editors, *Li Ch'ing Chao, Complete Poems,* New Directions Publishing Corp. 80 Eighth Ave, New York, 1979.

Seagrave, Sterling, *The Soong Dynasty*, Harper & Rowe, New York 1986.

Seagrave, Sterling, *Dragon Lady*, Alfred A. Knopf, New York, 1992.

Shen Che & Lu Xiaoya, *Life Among the Minority Nationalities of Northwest Yunnan*, editor Liao Pin, translator Huang Wei-wei, Foreign Language Press, Beijing 1989.

Shu Shiung, *Wang Chao Ch'un, Beauty in Exile*, Kelly & Walsh, Shanghai, 1934.

Sketches of Enterprising Women, Beijing, 1990.

Soong Ch'ing Ling, edited by Soong Ch'ing Ling Foundation, published by China Reconstructs, distributed by China International Book Trading Corp. Beijing, 1984.

Spence, Jonathan D., *The Search for Modern China*, W. W. Norton & Co.

New York & London, 1990.

Show, Edgar, *Red Star Over China*, Grove Press Inc. N.Y. 1938.

Terrill, Ross, *The White Boned Demon*, William Morrow & Co., Inc., New York 1984.

Vare, Daniele, *The Last of the Empresses*, John Murray, London, 1936.

Wang, Chia-Yu, *Love and Lives of Chinese Emperors*, translated and adapted by T. C. T'ang, Mei Ya Publications, Inc., Taipei, Taiwan, 1972.

Wei Tang, *Legends and Tales from History*, China Reconstructs Press, Beijing 1984.

Witke, Roxanne, *Comrade Ching Ch'ing*, Little Brown & Co., Boston, 1977.

Women in Chinese Folklore, published by Women of China Press, Beijing, 1983.

Magazine Articles

China Pictorial, #11, 1980 - *The Naxi People of Lugu Lake.*

China Pictorial #1, 1981, *China's Minority People, Songs, Dances and Photographs.*

China Pictorial #3, 1981, *Soong Ching Ling and her Times*, by Israel Epstein

China Pictorial #8, 1981, I*n Deep Memory of Soong Ching Ling, A Great Woman of Our Times.*

Nexus, China in Focus, *Woman Artist Develops a New Style of Folk Clay Sculpture*, China Bridge Magazine Co., Spring edition, 1980.

Nexus, China in Focus, *Woman Artist, Zhang Runzi*, CNH, Beijing, Spring 1990.

Renditions , A Chinese-English Translation Magazine, #32 special sections on Bing Xin and Li Ch'ing Chao, Research Centre for Translation, Chinese University of Hong Kong, Condor Productions Ltd., H.K., Autumn 1989.

Vanity Fair, *The Last Days of Madame Mao*, by Roxanne Witke, December 1991.

Women of China, #12, 1980. *Clay Figurines of Zhang Shumin*, Photographer Li Jiangshu.

Women of China, March 1988, *Women in Politics, Sketch of Shi Meiying, Director of Beijing #3 State Cotton Textile Mill* including a front cover picture of her. Script by Wang Xiaoming, Soong Ch'ing Ling Foundation, published by China Reconstructs, distributed by China International.

ISBN 155212381-2